Disclaimer: The author is not licensed to practice law or offer legal advice in any way. Nothing written herein is to be construed as such and is for information only. Any legal questions should be directed to an attorney.

Data and statistics have been taken from reliable media and reference sources. Where possible, credit has been given to these sources. We are not responsible for errors or information that has changed since their original publishing.

TABLE OF CONTENTS

Prologue

Prologue

This publication will provide the most comprehensive information that you will need as a citizen about to be indicted or already arrested by the Federal Government.

We have conducted more than 1000 hours of research into Criminal Law, Citations, Appeals and procedures and interviewed more than 200 convicted felons in various State and Federal Criminal Justice jurisdictions. Their charges run the gamut from white collar "crimes", "drug "kingpins", distributors/users/manufacturers, assaults, felon in possession, bank robbery, mail and wire fraud, tax evasion, murder and many more.

We have authored over 150 articles and newsletters on a variety of subjects, many related to government shenanigans and abuses. This is but another exposing the Criminal Justice System of The Department of Justice primarily related to THE PEOPLE OF THE UNITED STATES v. JOHN Q. PUBLIC (you). Some information will be applicable to charges brought about by the State in which you were charged but the preponderance will be related to charges brought about by the Federal Government against you.

This is the definitive guide through the legal minefield that you will find daunting by any standard of measure if you have never been subjected to it. Justice is not blind and the deck is stacked in this game.

The United States Government is all powerful, unforgiving and unrelenting in their pursuit of "justice"! They will extract their pound of flesh and attempt to destroy you financially at every opportunity.

Never forget Ruby Ridge and Waco!

On April 19, 1993 the United States Government, acting under Attorney General Janet Reno, sent FBI agents, ATF agents and the U.S. military and used cyanide gas and a flammable chemical disbursed from a tank against The Branch Davidians. Multiple snipers and heavy firepower were used to emolliate and murder 86 men, women and children at the "compound" in Waco, Texas.

None of the murdered had committed any crime before the Government wanted to make an example out of them, similar to Randy Weavers family at Ruby Ridge.

After Congressional investigation and a number of hearings conducted under Senator Diane Feinstein not one agent or Law Enforcement official was ever charged with a crime for those murders!

Regardless, an independent jury later found that that the Branch Davidians at Waco acted in self-defense against the illegal Government intrusion. Of course, it didn't matter then. They were all dead!

The United States Government cannot "grant freedom". It can only take it away!

Randy Weaver of Ruby Ridge fame was acquitted of all charges bought by the Government against him. Of course, by then, his wife, child and dog were already murdered by FBI sniper Lon Horiuchi and Randy had spent 18 months in jail awaiting trial and verdict! Later, Randy and his infamous attorney, Montana's Gerry Spence sued the Government civilly for their illegal activities and murders and won an unprecedented multi-million dollar award!

Chapter 1

THE UNITED STATES GOVERNMENT IS NOT YOUR FRIEND!

If you have served prison time on multiple occasions for criminal activity you may or may not find the information herein useful. You are cognizant of the system that you already know and the great risk that you face!

For those who are newbie's and perhaps had simple misdemeanor charges of traffic or some other minor offense brought against you this is a vital publication.

Remember.....Laws are made to be broken. When there aren't enough criminals we make them! Who wants a nation of law abiding citizens? There is nothing for anyone in that.

Passing laws that can neither be observed, enforced or objectively interpreted creates a nation of lawbreakers and then the powers that be can cash in on the "guilt"!

In *Constitutional Chaos* written by former **Judge Andrew Napolitano** he states the following:

- **The Government prosecutes individuals <u>it knows</u> is innocent**, seizes property from unwilling and unsuspecting citizens and "flips it" to curry favor!
- The Government lies, cheats and steals to enforce its own laws, yet does not obey the law itself.
- The Supreme Court no longer upholds the tenets of law or the Constitution.
- The Supreme Court condones deceit and lies and misrepresentation of facts by Law Enforcement to arrest and charge any person, guilty or not!
- "Custody" is an issue that the Courts use to determine whether questioning requires Miranda or not. *Custody*, like *Intent* or *Conspiracy* mean whatever the Prosecutor or Courts want it to mean, always in their favor!

This is from a Judge who spent many years on the bench!

- *The Law is not about TRUTH. It is about negotiation, amelioration and manipulation!*

- *The Law is not about guilt or innocence!*

- *The Law is not about Justice!*

The Law is simply about winning or losing!

One only has to look at the CRIMINAL JUSTICE "SYSTEM" to see a multitude of employment opportunities; Lawyers, Judges, Prosecutors, Assistant Attorney Generals, Paralegals, Clerks, Corrections Officers, Marshals, Police, Sheriffs, Counselors, Psychiatrists, Psychologists, Food Services, Politicians, Jailers, Investigators, Accountants, Researchers,

Probation and Parole
Officers, and many, many more!

Consider this in the Federal Criminal Justice "system".......................................

Attorney General	paid by the U.S. Government
U.S. Attorney	paid by the U.S. Government
Prosecutor	paid by the U.S. Government
Investigators	paid by the U.S. Government
Clerks	paid by the U.S. Government
Paralegals	paid by the U.S. Government
Secretaries	paid by the U.S. Government

YOUR FEDERAL PUBLIC DEFENDER..............paid by the U.S. Government!

Judges	paid by the U.S. Government....appointed for life!
Judges clerks	paid by the U.S. Government
Court reporters	paid by the U.S. Government
Marshals	paid by the U.S. Government
Paralegals, secretaries	paid by the U.S. Government
Probation/parole officers	paid by the U.S. Government

DEPARTMENT OF JUSTICE/TREASURY

FBI	paid by the U.S. Government
ATF	paid by the U.S. Government
DEA	paid by the U.S. Government

YOUR LAWYER.....................PAID BY YOU!

Think about it! **Your Government has unlimited funds and time while you spend upwards of $250.00 each and every hour your lawyer even thinks about your case.** You may be allowed to "bail out" awaiting disposition of your case. If not you will be incarcerated in some detention facility for up to two years before disposition of your case where you be separated from
your family, friends and will very likely lose your job.

If you have State charges brought against you rather than Federal charges there are some differences on how your case may be processed. For instance, a State charge will always result in a Preliminary Hearing unless this is waived by you.

The Preliminary hearing is sometimes called a Probable Cause Hearing and is the best opportunity to have the charges dropped and the case dismissed with prejudice (the government cannot re-file the same charges). Failing this first test will nearly always have results in moving into the process of mounting a defense.

Most states will not bring an indictment against you but will have a Preliminary Hearing after your Arraignment. .

Of course, this publication cannot possibly cover every nuance of the law, the legal process or every possible option that you may have to defend yourself nor is it designed to. Suffice it to say that you will find ample information here to make an intelligent decision on how you might want to proceed with your case.

It is important for you to understand that a "criminal" is simply anyone, but anyone who has broken the law. For example, jaywalking against a red light is against the law. By definition then, you are a criminal if you jaywalk. If you speed five miles over the speed limit in your vehicle you are a criminal. So criminals aren't always robbers, murderers, child molesters or bank robbers.

You, however, can easily be broad brushed with the stigma of being a "serious criminal" for merely being charged with a felony, no matter how minor.

The various Cities, States, Federal Government, United States Territories, Statutory Authorities have passed more than 25,000,000 (that's twenty five million) laws which exist today literally making each and everyone of us a "criminal" daily. This will be repeated as a reminder throughout this publication.

Should the government authorities wish to prosecute you, you could very well find yourself in the near helpless, hapless situation trying to defend yourself against overzealous prosecutors, and judges who likely share their desire to have you fined, imprisoned and placed on probation Probation is not likely in the Federal "System" until a release from prison custody after serving your sentence!

Chapter 2

FACTS THAT YOU MUST KNOW!

	1980	2010	Change
Population of U.S.A	227 million	310 million	**+30%**

PRISON POPULATION

States	305,000	1,800,000	**+500%**
Federal	24,300	202,000	**+900%**
Total	329,000	2,102,000	**+700%!**

Source: New York Times Almanac

Nearly very agency of the United States Government has significantly reduced employees from 1980 though 2010 except one. The Department of Justice has increased by 100% , from 56,300 to more than 125,000!

Some is attributable to the threat of terrorism, however, terrorist arrests in the U.S.A. or abroad are negligible compared to other "criminals" arrested in the United States; less than 1%! In other words, the Department of Justice has more than doubled to handle our new breed of criminal since the Reagan Administration which began to criminalize minor street crimes and begin THE WAR ON DRUGS in earnest!

Prisons Growth is serving 7.2 million clients!

By Darryl Fears
WASHINGTON POST

WASHINGTON- The number of people under supervision in the nation's criminal justice system rose to 7.2 million in 2006, the highest ever, costing states tens of billions of dollars to house and monitor offenders as they go in and out of jails and prisons.

According to a report released by the Bureau of Justice Statistics, more than 2 million offenders were in either jail or prison in 2006, the most recent year studied in an annual survey. An additional 4.2 million were on probation, and nearly 800,000 were on parole. A total of 10 million have been released who have served time for drug related charges

The cost to U.S.Government, about $45 billion, is causing states such as California to reconsider harsh criminal penalties. To relieve overcrowding, California is now exporting some inmates to privately run corrections facilities as far away as Tennessee.

"There are a number of states that have talked about an early release of prisoners deemed non-threatening," said Rebecca Blank, a senior fellow ill economic studies at the Brookings Institution, a centrist think tank. "The problem
just keeps getting bigger and bigger. You're paying a lot of money here. You have to ask if some of these high mandatory minimum sentences make sense."

The bureau's report comes on the heels of a Pew Center on the States report showing that 1 percent of U.S. adults are behind bars, a historic high. **The United States has the highest number of people behind bars in the world, according to the Pew report. (*By any standard of measure!*)**

Black men, about 1 in 15, were most affected, and Hispanics, 1 in 35, were heavily represented among offenders. The number of women in prison "rose faster in 2006 than over the previous five years," mostly in Hawaii, North Dakota, Wyoming and Oklahoma, the Bureau of Justice Statistics report said.

In 1980, about the time that tough sentencing laws, particularly for drug offenses, began to be passed by federal and state legislators, 1.8 million people were in the "system" and $ 1 billion was spent on corrections .

"It's really like a runaway train," said Ryan King, policy analyst for the liberal Sentencing Project. "Nobody's taking a step back and asking where all these billions of dollars are going:" With so much overcrowding, King said, states "need billions of dollars to build enough beds to catch up to where they need to be." Defenders argue that the rise in the prison population means that more dangerous criminals have been taken off the streets.

"If you look at the fact that these are people who are committing a crime, creating a danger to the public..you can't look at it as wrong," said Scott Thorpe, chief executive of the California District Attorneys Association. "What is the appropriate number of people to be incarcerated to ensure public safety? I don't know if you can answer that."

(I can: 30% of all prisoners have been convicted of non-violent crimes, victimless crimes and present no harm to society in any way. That number is well over 200,000 inmates!)

State contracts with private prisons to house offenders grew by 6 percent, or about 6,000 inmates, the report said. Nearly 104,000 state and federal prisoners were in private institutions in 2006.

Citizens are being indicted, arrested, convicted, sentenced and imprisoned for "crimes" that never were prosecuted or even existed 50 years ago!

White collar, "Victimless and Drug Crimes represent more than 70% of all arrests in the United States!

The United States of America is a Corporation! Every citizen is an "asset" to the United States Corporation beginning at birth.

In theory, the Corporation of the United States of America has no jurisdiction outside the limits of Washington D.C.. Yet, over time, the Corporation of the United States of America has infringed upon the property, rights and life of its' citizens and States without so much as a whimper.

Also, in theory, the Corporation of the United States of America can only sue anyone by Tort Law because they are a Corporation. They should only be able to charge anyone with CRIME within the limits of Washington D.C.!

The Corporation of the United States of America, through charade and a number of other subterfuges brings Criminal and Statutory Criminal charges against more than a quarter of a million citizens each and every year! These are bought through Federal Grand Jury indictments, arrests made by the Federal Bureau of Investigation, The Drug Enforcement Administration (DEA), The Food and Drug Administration (FDA), The Department of Treasury (Alcohol, Tobacco, Firearms and Explosives {ATF}) and a whole plethora of other agencies including local law enforcement.

The U.S.A. Corporation creates high theater by claiming that they have the authority and power to circumvent their own laws to arrest and prosecute its' citizens. By virtue of the fact that they do this every day gives credence to their nefarious acts. Remember this, any act or statement left unchallenged or unopposed becomes fact under law and tacit permission to continue!

The U.S.A. Corporation has been bankrupt since the 1930's and is now controlled by the "Trustees" of the bankruptcy, International Bankers. These International Bankers forced the implementation of the FEDERAL RESERVE BOARD or CENTRAL BANK upon the Congress of the United States in 1913. What has this got to do with you? EVERYTHING!

The JURISDICTION Chapter provides more information on this subject.

Nearly all Charges brought by the Federal Government against you come from a U.S. Attorney who presented evidence to a Grand Jury. In nearly every instance the Grand Jury is a rubber stamp for the U.S. Attorney. Those instances where a Grand Jury will not bring back a "True Bill" leading to your arrest or formal charges being brought against you are so rare as to non-existent!

There are more than **25,000,000 laws** that the government can enforce at their choosing. Worse yet, the Congress of the United States makes more than 3,000 laws each and every year, most of which no-one has ever heard of. Granted, most are not related to Criminal Law but many are. Even the lawyer that you may eventually hire may not know anything about the law under which your charges have been brought. You will be paying him to research your charges and the law to mount a defense before he can even start to help you.

- **97% of all Indictments lead to a conviction one way or another!**

THERE ARE 2,300,000 PERSONS SERVING A PRISON SENTENCE AS YOU READ THIS! 200,000+ are in one of the 114 Federal prisons located throughout the United States. There are more than 350,000 waiting for disposition on their cases. The remainder are in State facilities ranging from Detention centers to County jails to State prisons.

- **There is no longer Parole in the Federal prison system.**

Every convicted felon must serve at least 85% of their sentence. They can get even more time than that if they lose any or all of their 15% good time allocated upon the date of start of sentence imposed. The prisons are burgeoning with convicted felons due to the Sentencing Guidelines and Mandatory Sentences required under the old law.

We are not only a nation of laws but a nation of criminals what with the new laws created by Congress, overzealous Prosecutors and the Sentencing guidelines imposed by the High Priest Judges!

States still have a Parole program. It is possible for an exemplary inmate to serve less than half of their sentence under a State conviction.

There are **10,000,000 convicted felons already released from prison who have served their time on some sort of drug charge**.

There are another **4,000,000 released convicts on probation or parole** for other charges, not drug related!

One in thirty (1 in 30) Americans either are in prison or have been in prison. The number will get larger every year! 30% of these have committed victimless "crimes" with no foul, no harm to persons, property or assets.

Only 4% of Appeals on convictions are remanded back to the lower court for review. Some of those remanded back to lower court even result in a harsher sentence being than originally imposed!

The Supreme Court receives thousands and thousands of Appeals each year. The Court reviews a mere 80 or so. A chance that your Appeal might be heard is likely to be nil.

The President of the United States has the power to pardon or commute a convicted felons sentence. Interestingly, he cannot pardon anyone until they have been released for five years. He can, however, commute anyone's sentence while that person is still serving his/her sentence. Thousands of prisoners and released felons have petitioned the President to have their sentences pardoned or commuted. In any Presidential term the most that have acted been acted upon by a sitting President is less than 600, and most only pardon a couple of hundred!

These facts are not meant to discourage you!

By the time that you finish with this you will be able to better understand how you might win your case, or at the very least, lower fees, costs, time and sentence.

As you proceed through this guideline you will find information not normally found in such a publication. At times it may not seem to follow any particular order. In the end, however, a full cohesive understanding will be your reward.

Repetitiveness from chapter to chapter is to your benefit. It will serve as emphasis to remind you of an issue, process or procedure. Remember, nothing more will affect your life than being caught up the Federal Criminal Justice System!

Chapter 3
"Congress shall pass no law........."
(Constitution and Bill of Rights- an illusion)

"The United States is a nation of laws." We have heard that many times throughout our lives. You will find as you read on that we are most certainly a nation of laws, more than we can possibly obey!

The United States Government passes more than 3,000 laws per years as noted earlier. Many are designed, not so much to protect us from others, but to infringe more and more on our rights as citizens.

In the course of time many laws were passed by Congress to target specific individuals, groups or type of crime to stem the tide of violence, corruption or fraud. The National Firearms Act of 1934, 26 U.S.C. §5845 came about as a result of the so-called Italian mafia's violence over protecting territories and maximizing profits. The "sawed off shotgun" became illegal at the same time because it could be easily hidden in a trench coat or jacket with ballistics that are nearly impossible to trace.

Later, other laws came about such as RICO and certain Internal Revenue Service codes to bring down Criminal Enterprises The IRS is a private entity which operates under the color of law and has a code of STATUTES which the Government has illegally given them. The IRS has full authority of investigation and arrest of any citizen that they suspect has violated their Statutes.

The IRS operates under the jurisdiction of the Department of Treasury and works hand and glove with the Bureau of Alcohol, Tobacco, Firearms and now Explosives who also reports to the Department of Treasury.

The list is unending. Law libraries in every university offering law degrees has buildings that are chock full of law books, cases, rulings of courts, precedence's, appeals and a whole plethora of legal mumbo jumbo. These writings govern our lives each and every day and literally puts each and everyone of us at risk of being a criminal.

There are, of course, needs for new laws having to deal with new technologies and potential harm from new products, processes and other issues never addressed before.

But more and more "Criminals" are created with the passage each and every year of new criminalizing laws. As the prison population has grown ten fold over the last 20 years it would seem that we have ten times the amount of "criminals" than we did 20 years ago.

This can be attributed to three very important causes.

1. Laws have been passed since the Reagan Administration which have "criminalized"

many street crimes that were once considered misdemeanors or low grade felonies. These citizens are now being sentenced to Federal prison.

2. Mandatory Sentences and later Sentencing to the "Guidelines" have created a growth industry for the prison systems across America as convicted felons spend more time in prison and more others become incarcerated.

3. Parole has been eliminated from the Federal System. Parole often allowed convicted felons to serve as little as 50% of his time before release to Probation. Now, every convicted felon must serve 85% of his sentence compounding prison crowding and incarceration rates.

Still, Congress passes more and more laws, pressing the limits of the Constitution and Bill of Rights which have clearly been re-defined by the Courts in America and the Supreme Court itself! The Rights of John Q. Citizen that our grandparents enjoyed no longer exist for you today.

When one considers how much time a Congressman spends in Washington D.C. actually doing any work the Congressman actually has just enough time to read any bill for 30 minutes! Most of these bills are more than 500 pages long! His non-elected staff actually does all of the work formulating law, adding the earmarks and pork.

Wall Street Bankers and Brokers have pillaged the United States economy with near impunity! These "White Collar Crimes" will never, as a whole, even see a courtroom, much less a prison sentence unless the Government takes a token few for show.

After all, these bankers are largely responsible for the election of our Congressmen, Senators and even the President! They represent some of the largest Lobbyists in Washington, wining and dining our elected and making certain that their agendas are carried out.

Moreover, our unelected who run everything behind the scenes, including the NGO's (Non-Government Organizations), who survive all elections and stay throughout several administrations, create all of the Laws to protect their interests and eliminate their competition.

Who funds much of the campaigns of our elected? Who provides perks, vacations and siphons money into the secret bank accounts of our elected and their families? Of course it the Bankers and Brokers on Wall Street and large Corporate Government Contractors and the Media.

No one elected to office ever left office poorer than he went in, that's all you need to know! Occasionally, the Feds will Indict and Arrest a few sacrificial lambs during any term to give John Q. Citizen the impression that our elected are not immune from the law as they are accused of "misconduct" or taking "bribes". The Government will, from time to time, go after the unelected "advisors" and lobbyists who have given bribes, gratuity and other benefits to curry favor from Congressmen.

Just as the Feds will do the same with Crime "Kingpins" which get widespread media coverage while our corrupt officials blithely continue to pass more laws to reduce our freedoms even further.

But if **you (John Q. Citizen)** write a bad check or file a tax return with errors and the Government decides that it wants to make a case against you they will prosecute you to the fullest extent of the law.

Federal Prisons have a sizable population of those who have committed financial crimes. Of course the law may have been broken but the sentences are far askew of the "crime" committed, thanks to the Lawyers and their staff in Congress who create these laws and the Department of "InJustice" who designs the sentences! The Federal Government does not want John Q. Public, especially Joe Six Pack, screwing around with the money.

The United States Government regularly violates its own laws with impunity. Laws are passed by Congress which violate the spirit and intent of the Constitution. Actions taken by Government officials, Government Law Enforcement and Government employees violate the law every day.

The daily news constantly reminds us of the crime and corruption prevalent in Government, both State and Federal. Very few Government employees or officials are prosecuted for these "indiscretions"! Those that are given more than a modicum of attention to make the public believe that the Government is not above the law. A few sacrificial lambs are thrown to the lions to make an example of them, while the entire system is corrupt through and through.

The real reason behind overcrowding in prisons

By Anthony Gregory
GUEST COMMENTARY

IN RESPONSE to a crisis of massive prison overcrowding, Gov. Schwarzenegger has called for the construction of two more prisons.

Since 1980, the state of California has built more than 20 prisons, and its prison population has increased about fivefold. With about 170,000 inmates, it has a higher per-capita incarceration rate than the rest of the United States, which itself has the highest per-capita prison population in the industrialized world.

This is all good news for law enforcement unions and politicians. From the public's point of view, however, it is not so positive.

In a typical example of the failure of imprisonment, we see that no matter how many prisons are built, no matter how much money the politicians throw at the problem, there is overcrowding.

Conditions for prisoners deteriorate. Rape and brutality have become the norm.

The most obvious reform is almost never mentioned: Stop locking up so many people and start letting a lot of people out. Surely America isn't the most criminal culture on earth. Why does the United States have the most prisoners? The main reason is too many laws.

More prisoners are locked away for drug violations than all violent crimes combined. It used to be perfectly legal for anyone to walk into a store and buy heroin or cocaine. Then the progressives took over in the early 20th century and began waging a war on drugs, which blossomed under Franklin Roosevelt's New Deal, when marijuana became nationally illegal.

People have a right to liberty,

Surely America isn't the most criminal culture on earth. Why does the United States have the most prisoners? The main reason is too many laws.

property, and the pursuit of happiness. It is an affront to the founding principles of America to lock peaceful people into cages just because they consume or sell drugs.

It is also ineffective in reducing drug abuse. And it leads to more violent crime, gang warfare, judicial and police corruption, and all the other problems that accompanied alcohol prohibition.

Those who have committed no crime against person or property should be released from the jails and prisons. These include drug offenders, sex workers, those in possession of illegal guns, and anyone else who has hurt and threatened no one, whose only offense was to violate a victimless crime statute.

At a cost of about $35,000 per inmate per year, not only is keeping them in prison enormously expensive, draining resources that could be used to pursue actual violent criminals, but it is downright immoral.

As for minor property criminals, justice should be about making the victim whole, not about expensively caging people just to provide jobs for the prison guards, money for the bureaucracy, and talking points for tough-on-crime politicians.

Instead of being forced to pay taxes that go to jailing their offenders, victims should at least have the option of being reimbursed for what was stolen from them and compensated for their trouble.

Moving toward a restitution model would free up valuable space. So would stopping the overzealous enforcement of Three Strikes against people whose third strike was a minor, nonviolent offense.

Critics have accused Schwarzenegger of being too close to the prison guard lobby. Of course, Gray Davis wasn't exactly the lobby's enemy. Both Republicans and Democrats love the prison industrial complex.

It was Davis, in fact, who angered much of the left when he invited the corporations in to benefit from low-cost labor.

Whereas in a free market, businesses have to pay their employees an adequate wage or the employees can quit and go elsewhere, the corporate state provides a literally captive labor market for industry, socializing the costs to the taxpayers.

As with so much else that government does, it is horrible for the economy on balance, but some people get fabulously wealthy from it. Here we see a lot of the incentive for more prisons.

America and especially California have a sickness right now, an addiction to prisons that distinguishes them as the great incarcerators of the world.

This will not do in a free country. It is corrupting our culture and bankrupting our economy, all to benefit the corporate state that profits in proportion to how many of us are in cages.

Right now, California is taking the lead in prison abuse. Instead, it should take the lead toward sensibility and freedom, and start releasing those prisoners who have violated the rights of no one.

The States compound the problem by passing laws within their own Legislatures. Often, States laws conflict with Federal Laws and sometimes the Constitutionality of either or both are taken to the Supreme Court for   disposition.

The Court was designed to be the Arbiter of those laws which may conflict with the Constitution and your Rights under that Constitution. The Supreme Court has become the new ipso facto revisionist organ as evidenced from their rulings over recent years. These rulings have clearly destroyed the spirit and intent of the Founders when they created this document that defines our Government, it's limits and their function.

The business of making laws has become a full time job and career for our lawyer lawmakers. For more than a hundred years various elected Senators and Congressman left their farming, banking, merchant and educational jobs to go to Washington **for a few months** and addressed the issues facing the country.

Now, most of these Lawyers spend every year, for nearly the full year, conjuring ways how to expropriate as much money as it can from you and business and wherever they can find another dollar for their pet "projects" and entitlements to give to their benefactors, the lazy and illegals.

When they aren't doing that they are constantly campaigning for their next election so that they can do the same thing over and over again. The government has turned into a self perpetuating machine of good old boys who could care less about the citizens of the United States except for your money and your vote.

This condemnation doesn't do much to help your case but it may clarify to you how insignificant your plight is to the Government who claims to represent the "People" against you.

Chapter 4

Law Enforcement

Just because you're paranoid doesn't mean they're not out to get you!

With so many laws on the books it is axiomatic that these laws must be enforced. Of course, it is impossible to enforce **every** law. Most are obsolete. Some are obscure. Federal Criminal Laws under Title 18 and those that fall under other Title and Statutes are those that are applicable here.

To assure that society is protected from "criminals" a myriad of Law Enforcement agencies exist.

City Police: The front line law enforcement agency in America. While traffic represents a large portion of their activity to generate revenue they apprehend the most criminals.

Police officers report to superior ranks who, then , in turn report to a Police Chief. The Police Chief is appointed by the City Mayor sometimes with the approval of the City Counsel. When a city being governed day to day by a City Manager he will approve the nomination of a Police Chief and the Chief will report to the City Manager and City Council.

County Sheriffs: The Sheriff is the highest, most powerful law enforcement agent in the United States. Why? Because he is the only **elected** law Enforcement agent in the country!

His power is so complete that, if he chose to, he could keep every Federal Agent out of his county without specific written permission from his office! Few, if any, County Sheriffs exercise this power, but they should.

The Sheriff and his Deputies are generally responsible for Law Enforcement outside of City limits, acting as bailiffs in courtrooms (counterpart to U.S. Marshals in the Federal venue), securing the County jails and transporting inmates.

State Police: Usually report to the Governor and largely traffic control on State Highways. They have investigative authority and arrest many criminals as a result of their traffic stops and searches.

THE FEDERAL GOVERNMENT RELIES LARGELY ON LOCAL LAW ENFORCEMENT TO DISCOVER A LARGE NUMBER OF CRIMES THAT CAN FALL UNDER FEDERAL JURISDICTION.

While the **Federal Bureau of Investigation** employs some 35,000, 12,000 are acting field agents dealing with every crime imaginable. Unless an individual or group has been targeted for investigation as a result of their ideology, suspected crimes or threats **the FBI generally "selects" White Collar "criminals" to investigate and arrest.**

Agents of the FBI report to their SAC (Special Agent in Charge) of their assigned offices in various cities. They, in turn report to a district supervisor who reports to a superior in Washington D.C.. The chain of command goes to Assistant Directors and then to the Director of the FBI. The Director reports to the Attorney General of the United States, appointed by the President.

In addition, the Government is loaded with various and sundry "Alphabet" soup of Agencies to surveillance, investigate and arrest.

The DEA (Drug Enforcement Agency). **The ATF** (Alcohol, Tobacco and Firearms and Explosives). **The Secret Service** (Protecting the President and chasing Counterfeiters), **U.S. Customs, Border Patrol, Immigration and Naturalization Service.** NSA(National Security Agency). **The United States Marshals Service.** Department of Agriculture (yes, these have arrest authority under the Department of the Interior; Fish and Game, FEMA, Forestry Service and more).

Topping all of these now we have **HOMELAND SECURITY** which has sweeping authority over all the above listed agencies and others. If the Government decides that you represent a threat to National Security by your words, writings, purchases or associations you will fall under their close scrutiny.

The Patriot Act of 2003 and reaffirmed last year all but suspends your Constitutional Rights if the Government targets you for investigation. You may be detained for an indeterminate period of time without a formal arrest, indictment or charges . You may or may not be allowed to talk to an attorney on a timely basis. You will not be allowed visitation of any kind. You could be held for months while the Government builds a case against you and you may not even know that you have committed a "crime"! Impossible? It happens every day in these United States of America!

The U.S. Attorney for any District in the United States has a number of Assistant U.S. Attorney's who actually Prosecute criminal who have been charges. They have investigative powers and unlimited resources with which to pursue indictments and authorize arrests through he Courts.

Throughout this publication when the term Prosecutor is used, it means U.S. Attorney or his Assistants.

The term, Federal Government, means Congress, the U.S. Attorney, his Assistants and any Law Enforcement agency such as the FBI, ATF, DEA, etc..

Chapter 5

Drugs, Controlled substances
Why First and Foremost?

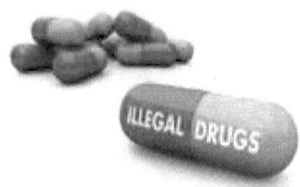

70% of all inmates in prisons have been convicted under some DRUG CHARGE!

Ten million (10,000,000) felons have served time for a Drug crime and are on Probation, Parole or fully released in America today!

The media would have you believe that these "drug" arrests are all major "dealers" and "distributors", a menace to society. As it turns out the vast majority of these convictions are related to the growth and use of marijuana. To argue the pros and cons of the laws that make this possible is not the point here. The fact is, it is against the law to grow, use or sell marijuana.

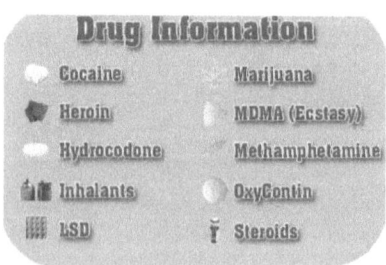

- *Unless you were caught "red handed" with drugs as a result of a traffic stop and search, seen actually doing a transaction or otherwise found with some sort of "drug" you have been part of an investigation for some time.*

- *It is likely that someone that you know well has told authorities that you use, buy or have sold drugs in the past or are now engaged in that activity. He or she did this in the hopes and expectation that their charges will be reduced or forgiven for providing this information. The more individuals caught in the "criminal enterprise" as a result of informants the better the informants "deal".*

Your name may have been given to authorities just because someone knows someone who might have mentioned your name at one time or another. You may never have been

involved with drugs or lightly used at a party just once. The authorities do not care. They have your name and you will be charged and could be convicted simply for this one indiscretion!

If the authorities can find a phone record or one other witness against you where there was a connection between you and the primaries in the investigation you will likely go to prison! Sometimes they don't even need that.

- *Law enforcement and the Prosecutor <u>will</u> "stack" charges on the drug charge to assure a conviction by you "pleading out" (pleading guilty to a lesser charge) or overwhelming the jury in a trial with so much legal gobbledygook they cannot do anything else but bring back a guilty verdict.*

Here's how it works. Drugs may or may not be found in your possession.

- *If they searched your house or vehicle legally or illegally and found drugs....or....*
- *If they found a beaker, glassware, Drano, gasoline, ammonia, acid, alcohol...or....*
- *If they "heard" that you, at one time or another used, bought or sold drugs....or....*
- *If they can tie you with a phone record to any known drug seller, user..............or....*
- *If anyone said they saw you once or more using or selling or buying..............or...*
- *They have you an tape or video actually planning or doing a drug "deal"......or...*

Getting the idea?

The authorities can and usually add charges from the Criminal Code like:

- *Conspiracy (means anything that the Government wants it to mean!)*
- *<u>Intent</u> to commit conspiracy, believe it or not! (Government can foretell the future)*
- *Conspiracy with Intent to Distribute (See above)*
- *Conspiracy with intent to Manufacture (as in the case with meth)*
- *<u>Intent</u> to manufacture (believe it or not!)*
- *<u>Attempted</u> possession, believe it or not! (Government can read your mind!)*
- *Part of a Criminal Enterprise - or RICO (A bunch a guys regularly doing "crime")*
- *Interfering with Interstate Commerce (This is the catch-all "crime"!)*
- *Money laundering (frequent or large deposits and withdrawals from a bank)*
- *Quantities or weight of drugs found (sometimes exceeding what they really found)*

And woe to you if a firearm of any kind is found where you have access to it, called "Dominion and Control" of that firearm.

That becomes the weapon used in the commission of a crime. The crime of the Drug Trade that you are accused of being engaged in and will add several years to the sentence should you be found guilty!

The more firearms that you have "Dominion and Control" over the higher that sentence will be.

- *You may have legal recourse to prevent any evidence against you found in your vehicle after a traffic stop from being used against you! You must act quickly after your arrest, preferable during the Arraignment process to have this "evidence" suppressed. Here is how certain courts have ruled.*

  If, for example, a law enforcement officer (local, state, Federal) has asked you to leave your vehicle and subsequently restrained you with handcuffs either in his vehicle or by his vehicle

  -And-

  began to search your vehicle without your permission (NEVER, NEVER, NEVER GIVE PERMISSION) and found something incriminating that he would not be able to see otherwise, he has conducted an illegal search and whatever might be found that might incriminate you cannot be used against you!

THE OFFICER MUST HAVE "PROBABLE CAUSE" to search your vehicle after a stop and restraint. By being restrained you already have been searched and pose no further threat to the officer, nor could you have tampered with any clearly observable "evidence" that might be used against you, therefore, you no longer have access to your vehicle where a weapon or other threat to the officer may be available to you. This also could be argued if you were apprehended outside of your residence.

Be advised, however, that if the officer sees or smells alcohol, the odor of "weed" , that your coherency is impaired or that there is clearly something visible in your vehicle by simple observation, these are actionable items that can result in a valid argument for PROBABLE CAUSE. Whatever evidence found and statements made regarding that evidence at the scene can and will be used against you!

However, law enforcement is not legally allowed to go on a "fishing expedition" to see what they can find without a PROBALE CAUSE WARRANT issued by affidavit to a sitting judge.

All bets are off, however, if, as a result of your traffic stop law enforcement has found outstanding warrants for you on their "Want and Make" NCIC search under your name or the vehicle registration. You are, in essence, a fugitive under that Warrant and certain aspects of your "Rights" no longer exist. A search will be conducted and, while you may argue later that the search was illegal, you are not likely to get a favorable ruling from the court to withhold anything found that could be used against you to enhance your charge(s).

*The government will confiscate any and all assets that **they believe** were attained through what they define as a Criminal Enterprise. Again, a Criminal Enterprise can mean anything the Government wants it to mean! They will freeze bank accounts, take stocks, bonds and anything else that they can find, and they can find anything of record through illegal searches!*

They will confiscate vehicle, boats, tools, jewelry, home(s), cash and anything else of value pending the outcome of their prosecution whether you are guilty or not! Even if you are released soon after apprehension you may not get back anything that was confiscated by Law

Enforcement!

You must move quickly to have these assets protected, moved or otherwise preserved as soon after indictment or arrest as possible. Trust no one but your closest confidants in this endeavor. You will pay your lawyer serious money to have him work through the process to have your possessions and assets returned and he may not be successful anyway!

A WORD ON ALCOHOL AND THE GOVERNMENTS "WAR ON DRUGS"!

In 1919 the United States Congress passed something called the *Volstead Act*. It became known as THE NATIONAL PROHIBITION ACT. In its infinite wisdom the U.S. Government attempted to legislate morality and America's alcohol consumption. This law prohibited anyone from manufacturing alcohol in volume, from consuming alcohol in establishments and from selling alcohol except for scientific purposes.

In one fell swoop of a pen a large percentage of Americans became law breakers overnight. These individuals had hoarded alcohol or began to frequent the newly established "Speakeasy's" that sprang up all over major cities. Payoffs to law enforcement authorities assured continued business for these Speakeasy's. Those who wouldn't co-operate were raided and arrests made until the owners fell back into line with the payoffs.

Worse, this law created a whole new breed of criminal as it became apparent that Americans were still going to consume their alcoholic beverages. These new "criminals" began to distill and import alcohol from every source that they could find in Canada, Mexico and Great Britain. The price of alcohol skyrocketed but people continued to buy, just as they do with drugs today.

For 13 years this law was in effect and during that time the violence on the streets of New York, Philadelphia, Chicago and other major cities became a near nightly occurrence as Italian, Irish and Jewish "gangs" struggled for territory and profits! Sound familiar?

Many multi-millionaires were created from Volstead Act as a result of their criminal activities, not just the "Gangster"!

Joe Kennedy, the Patriarch of the famous Kennedy clan made his fortune illegally importing alcohol. Armand Hammer, Uncle of former President Al Gore, the Jew former Chairman of Occidental Petroleum and Communist sympathizer began his fortune by using alcohol in other flavored medicinal products. Those are the most notable that come to mind. There were hundreds of others.

Today, the Courts have ruled in certain cases that a prior conviction of a DUI, regardless of the circumstances, have put you in the category of a "violent criminal" or having committed violent crime! As preposterous as this sounds it is indicative of how the courts will got to any length to win convictions and impose heavier sentences.

The lesson in all of this? The Government regularly makes criminals of otherwise law abiding citizens simply by passing legislation or the Courts regularly interpreting laws jeopardizing the freedoms of the American Public. All of this in the interest of preventing serious crime or certain groups of individuals to continue their criminal enterprise.

Consider this: The Government has recently passed the new HEALTH CARE bill.

Included in the fine print of this NATIONAL HEALTH CARE bill are clauses which require that every qualified person "contribute" to the cost by mandatory "purchasing" insurance annually.

Enforcement for this required "purchase" will fall under the Internal Revenue Service (IRS) jurisdiction. Failure to "purchase" this insurance can and will result in fines and imprisonment! The public had no say, no vote and is in jeopardy of losing their freedom if they do not comply with this new law!

Along the way, Law Enforcement makes arrests under broad interpretation of their duties and overzealous Prosecutors prosecute these individuals "to the fullest extent of the law" which can mean anything the Prosecutor and the Courts want it to mean!

It is not by accident that almost 30% of all those incarcerated throughout these United States are non-violent, victimless "criminals" put in this confinement due to spurious law and interpretation! They have no business being incarcerated and yet, people like these are being arrested and convicted daily in the Courts throughout the country. You could be next, or maybe you already are!

The San Diego Union Tribune reported in 2008 on the effort to petition President Bush to commute the sentence of former Rep. Randy "Duke" Cunningham, who pleaded guilty in 2005 to accepting some $2-4 million in bribes. The president has the constitutional power to pardon federal offenders by wiping clean their prison records for sentences served or by commuting the sentences of inmates in federal prison.

Before Bush even considers such a request, he ought to take a long look at the thousands of petitions for a presidential pardon filed by inmates who have never served in elective office. He could start with the case file of Clarence Aaron, who at age 23in 1992, while a student at Southern University in Baton Rouge, La., made the criminal decision to introduce two drug dealers, which resulted in a transaction **involving 9 kilograms of cocaine**.

Aaron broke the law, and the fitting consequence for that is a serious prison stay. But because Aaron was a newbie to the drug trade and did not have the experience with the criminal-justice system that would have led him to testify against the trade kingpins in exchange for a lighter sentence, and because his five co-conspirators knew enough to fess up and turn on him while he wrongly and stupidly denied any guilt, Aaron was handed the longest sentence in the group. He was **a first-time nonviolent drug offender but a judge sentenced him to life without parole.**

Having entered prison as a young man, he will die there unless a president pardons him. *(It is important to note that this man had exhausted every remedy available to him on appeals. The higher courts upheld the lower courts sentencing decision because all judges are in collusion to keep the prisons full. All judges belong to the same "fraternity" and will not act upon another's decision unless the facts are so glaringly public and outrageous)*

There is something rotten to the core in a justice system that puts a twenty something first-time nonviolent offender away for life, while **meting out lighter sentences for career criminals who know how to game the system**. Life without parole also is the same sentence imposed on FBI-agent-turned- Russian -spy Robert Hanssen, except that it is worse for Aaron, who was sentenced in 1992. arrested at age 56. It turns out Aaron's most heinous offense was not the drug deal, but not having spent years getting arrested and learning how to roll through the criminal justice machine. ,
John Overmyer / NewsArt

Up until the 1930's anyone could walk into a drug store and purchase as much cocaine and grow and smoke as much marijuana as they wanted. The original Coca-Cola (Coca= Cocaine) had cocaine in it until it was declared illegal!

These drugs became illegal as a result of the founding of the Food and Drug Administration (FDA) at the same time. The FDA controls much of the Medical, Pharmaceutical and Food industry with a fist of iron even though it actually operates under Maritime Law (remember the 25,000,000 laws in America).

Methamphetamine and a whole plethora of other DRUGS are illegal as we all know so well from the media attention it gets and the numbers of convicted drug felons whiling away in prisons across the country.

The government particularly doesn't want John Q. Public involved with marijuana and Meth because these DRUGS can be cultivated or manufactured by ANYONE! Cocaine and Opium (Heroin, Morphine) are DRUGS that are harvested in other countries and require a sophisticated network to smuggle into the United States. That is, unless you are the United States Government. They are the largest "importers" (read smugglers) of drugs anywhere!

The reason that the government is so harsh on our own homegrown varieties of drugs is that you are eating into the **INTERNATIONAL DRUG TRADE** sanctioned by the government. They want you on **their** drugs, paying them instead of your friend or dealer down the street who has his cottage industry of growing marijuana or manufacturing drugs (Meth, Ecstasy, etc.).

That is not to say that a large amount of weed and meth isn't coming across our borders. It is. These products are not generating revenue to the U. S. Government.

Remember, the Government is bankrupt and needs a steady supply of unaccountable cash to fund many off budget programs. Our foray into Viet-Nam and Afghanistan was and is largely to provide these unaccountable DRUG funds to the Government.

Manual Noriega was our drug conduit to the Columbian Cartels until he "skimmed" too much. While at the CIA George Bush 1 put Noriega in as El Presidente of Panama for this reason and took him out later for skimming too much when Bush became President of the United States! Bush invaded a sovereign foreign nation with Marines, laid siege to the Presidential Palace in Panama City and finally seized Emmanuel Noriega. He brought Noriega back to Florida where he was tried and convicted and sentenced to seventeen years in a Federal prison. Amazing! All the while the U.S. Government continued to smuggle drugs into this country using the military and private companies.

The next best thing is to impose Draconian sentences on those that they arrest, and arrest they do. More time, energy and dollars are spent by law enforcement to apprehend and arrest DRUG "DEALERS" than any other crime! Why! First, to give the impression that the United States Government is really concerned about the drug problem in America. Second, follow the money. The real idea is to remove the competition from the streets. How much money and drugs disappear after the arrest, on the way to the evidence room or disappears from the evidence room?

The drugging of America is an accomplished fact. Alcohol is passé now and drawing scorn from the media blitz with the intent to move the populous to drugs. DUI check points, Mothers Against Drunk Drivers, Rehabs, AA and an entire industry of social workers, counselors and interventionists has come into play to shame everyone who drinks.

The huge "busts" given large coverage by the press as the Border Patrol or Coast Guard discovers tons of ....pick a drug... are for show to lead the American to believe that we are serious about stemming the tide of drugs to the United States. After 30 years of the WAR ON DRUGS and millions of citizens sent to prison, the United States has more DRUGS and people using DRUGS than ever before.

The expectation that they will deter another from dealing is a farce because it simply makes the product more expensive   and attracts more to the "trade".

Moreover, the Government is part and parcel to the Drug Industry's mantra..."A pill for every malady". The Government wants the public on drugs, especially the psychotropic or mind altering kind. From cradle to grave we are bombarded with advertisements for some sort of drug by the Pharmaceutical Companies, all condoned and sanctioned by the Government!

Rarely does one hear of a driver being ticketed or arrested for being under the influence of "weed" or cocaine or heroine. You are asked to "blow" into the BAC machine for alcohol and, unless you give a blood or urine test you will not be found to have drugs in your system.

This is not a condoning of drinking and driving but the implication that alcohol is involved in so may traffic deaths or accidents belies the fact that in a large percentage of those statistics, the person not drinking caused the accident or death. It just so happens that the person who has alcohol in any amount in their system is either at fault or generates the statistic of "alcohol involved". The government wants you on drugs, not alcohol! They don't make nearly as much revenue on the tax on alcohol!

The FDA and pharmaceutical companies are constantly barraging us with advertising for their drugs. Depression, Sleep, Anxiety, etc., etc.. The worst of the worst is the drugging of our children because they are "hyperactive" or have "Attention Deficit Disorder". They see their parents taking one form or another of a pill and zone out. They are addicts before they reach puberty!

The advertisements for drugs are so prevalent you can't open a magazine or turn on the TV without seeing full page ads costing tens of thousands of dollars trying to get you to buy their DRUG!

Yet, nearly every one requires a Doctors prescription which he will gladly give you! And if the Drug is good enough (Oxycontin, Vicoden, Demerol, Valium and Percocet come to mind) these become street drugs sold at a premium for those who want to get high, low or die!

America will never be without DRUGS without a major cultural change about our mores and morality. What is the solution? More prisons? More Law Enforcement? More Courts? More Judges? More Prosecutors? More Rehabs? More hospitals?

Of course, legalizing all drugs will de-criminalize sellers and users and make them more cheaply available under controlled conditions. The United States is not ready to adopt this viable solution. Nonetheless, people who want to get high, get low or die will always use **SOMETHING** and there will be others to provide that **SOMETHING** as long as money can be made.

The cost to society is enormous in lost work, medical, theft, assaults, impaired decisions, break up of the family, death.

People who want to use will find their drug of choice somewhere. Arresting and removing "dealers" from the street only result in another taking their place.

When all is said and done DRUG DEALING is simply a BUSINESS!

Consider this:

With some glassware, heaters and cheap chemicals available at any grocery store and $40.00 worth of raw material starting at 7:00 AM; by 7:00 PM that very same day one person can convert pseudoephedrin (or the real stuff) into $1,400.00 of saleable "product"! That's 30X profit excluding labor which comes out to being paid over $100.00 per hour! By the way, that is just a one ounce "batch". Consider the enormous profits making a one pound "batch". And it takes no longer to manufacture than one ounce!

AND MORE:

A street dealer with little or no education can make more money in a month than an engineer or scientist or a college professor can make in a year!

Is it no wonder that the "War on Drugs" is lost, will never be won and that the laws, enforcement and associated costs are totally futile! Especially when the fact is that this street dealer just as often as not sells his product to that engineer, scientist and college professor!
....
....

THE METH CULTURE:

Methamphetamine use is rampant throughout the country today. Heavy users are called "Tweakers" . Meth results in chemical changes within the body and in the psyche of the user, severe and dangerous when used over long periods of time.

Meth becomes extremely addictive in as little as one use! It will keep the user awake for days at a time, reduce appetite and, after prolonged use, Tweakers will do nearly anything to get another "fix". It is not uncommon for them to break into automobiles for saleable items, steal whatever they can from them as well as the auto itself, commit burglary, lie, cheat or steal from family and friends to get enough money for their habit.

Over time, due to diet and the chemical itself, teeth will rot in the gums and discolor to a dark color, a sure sign of Meth use. Thought processes become confused and incoherent. Nervousness and erratic behavior are the norm. Unless this is checked the user can suffer Grand Mal seizures and even die. All the while believing that all he needs is another fix to get well.

Some experts claim that Meth is the most addictive drug ever to come on the scene in America. They could very well be right. It is the most potent of "highs", far exceeding cocaine.........and it is home grown (manufactured), easy to obtain and easy to "cook".
....
....

A drug charge can easily bring you a stiffer prison sentence than murder, especially in the State "System". Drug "kingpins" can get 20 years and a murderer will get less than 10! The government loves "Kingpins". These are identified as Drug Dealers who have a Distribution

Network where investigators have found that 3 or more individuals have purchased some sort of Drug from the "Kingpin". It makes for good headlines and gives the Prosecutors some real traction in their careers.

Nearly all drug charges brought against an individual are a result of someone informing ("snitching"/"narcking") on him. An arrest is made on an individual in possession of some drug and he is promised leniency if he tells where he bought the drugs and who else might be a seller. They, in turn will do the same and so on and so on until a case will be brought to the court with a multitude of co-defendants, many not knowing or ever seeing one another, ever!

Often, only one transaction ever took place and just out of curiosity. Being in the wrong place at the wrong time. A one minute transaction can land you three years in prison.

The more the drug the longer the sentence. And we're not talking tons here! The difference between a few grams of meth and a few ounces of meth is the difference between 18 months and 5 years. A pound or so can get you ten years. Cocaine and heroine are in a league all to themselves. The list in the sentencing guidelines is long and covers nearly every possible quantity, and the government is very specific about quantities!

Chapter 6

Indicted? Now What

The Federal Government is required to bring an Indictment for all capital and "infamous" crimes returned by a Grand Jury. This is required under the 5th Amendment of the Bill of Rights of the Constitution. **Over time this has been interpreted to mean that any Federal charge of a felony requires an Indictment returned by a Grand Jury.**

In each jurisdiction the Grand Jury meets in secret and no Attorney is present excepting the U.S. Attorney or Prosecutor. He/she presents "evidence" to the Grand Jury and the panel, consisting of up to 25 citizens that only need a majority vote to bring the Indictment.

An Indictment can be brought against a potential criminal or Criminal Enterprise without an arrest having been made. A simple investigation can result in sufficient evidence to be presented to the Grand Jury to bring an Indictment.

When a Grand Jury is satisfied with the evidence provided by the Prosecutor they issue a "True Bill" with which the Prosecutor can bring formal charges against the accused.

Grand Juries are commonly rubber stamps for prosecutor allegations, even with a modicum of evidence. Grand Juries regularly hear as many as ten cases per days and issue True Bills on every one of them.

If a felony arrest has been made the Prosecutor will still go the Grand Jury to make the formal accusation. If the Grand Jury "indicts" formal charges will then be bought against you along with any other the Assistant U.S. Attorney/Prosecutor can conjure up, thus "stacking" charges for the expected future Plea offer.

Subpoenas can be issued and witnesses can be called to testify at a Grand Jury proceeding and the targeted criminals often do not know that they have been Indicted or even investigated.

An indictment is not a finding of guilt! It is a formal accusation based upon evidence and testimony that a crime has been committed and now the U.S. Attorney or prosecutor can bring charges.

If a Grand Jury renders an Indictment and you are not already under arrest a warrant will be issued for your arrest. If you already have been arrested on the charges brought by the Government or the state you will be placed under a **DETAINER** which will be used to transfer you from one custody to the other when you are "disposed" of from the first.

It can happen that the Federal Government will take "jurisdiction" over the local or State authorities and move you to their jurisdiction while your other charges are pending.

Chapter 7

Arrested? Now what?
Habeas Corpus and other such nonsense

"You have the right to remain silent. Anything you say can and will be used against you in a court of law. You have the right to an attorney. If you cannot afford an attorney, one will be appointed to you. Do you understand these right as they have been explained to you?" (Miranda versus Arizona, 1966)

These are your extended 5th amendment rights against self incrimination after you are arrested. **Law Enforcement does not have tell you these rights if they DO NOT arrest you but merely detain you for questioning.** How you respond to their questioning may determine whether you will subsequently be arrested.

The various "White Collar Crimes" for which you can be arrested:

What are White Collar Crimes?

White collar crimes are a variety of non-violent crimes usually committed in commercial or business situations for financial gain. Most of these crimes are prosecuted by the federal government and are considered very serious in nature. The term "White collar" refers to the fact that people who commit these crimes are usually high-powered professionals, as opposed to "Blue-Collar" laborers.

Examples of White Collar Crimes
- ## Computer / Internet Fraud
    - Applying for credit cards online under false names
    - Unauthorized use of a computer or information on that computer
    - Manipulation of computer files
    - Computer sabotage / hacking

- **Bankruptcy Fraud**
    - Misleading creditors
    - Concealing assets from the bankruptcy court
- **Bribery**
    - Offering of money or anything of value which is used for the purpose of influencing the actions of the decision maker
- **Credit Card Fraud**
    - Unauthorized use of a credit card
    - Identity theft
- **Counterfeiting**
    - Coping or imitating an item without authorization with the intention to try and pass it off as the genuine article
    - This is mostly associated with money but can also apply to drivers' licenses, immigration papers, or any other important documents
- **Trade Secret Theft**
    - Theft or misappropriation of trade secret information
    - A trade secret is anything used in a business that makes them different, and for that secret to be exposed would cause the business to lose substantial value
    - An example of this would be for an employee of Coca-cola to leak their recipe to Pepsi and get paid for it
- **Health Care Fraud**
    - Usually has some relation to insurance and includes but is not limited to:
        - Kick backs
        - Billing for services not rendered
        - Billing for unnecessary equipment
        - Billing by a lesser qualified person - like a nurse billing under the hours of a doctor
        - Any kind of falsification of records to make an additional profit
- **Insider Trading**
    - Those with privileged information take special advantage and reap profits or avoid losses in the stock market to the detriment of the typical investor, however Jew bankers and brokers are responsible for stock market manipulations each and every day!
    - More information about securities law can be found at Securities Law
- **Anti-Trust Violations**
    - Attempts by one or two companies to dominate a particular market by getting rid of all competition.
    - More information about anti-trust violations can be found at Anti-trust and Trade Regulation

Remember, the U.S. Government does not want John Q. Public screwing with the money. Jew bankers and brokers are given a free ride.

What is Criminal Fraud?

Criminal Fraud is a White Collar Crime that includes anything intended to deceive, including all statements, acts, concealments, and omissions involving a breach of legal duty, trust or confidence, which results in injury to one who justifiably relies.

Criminal fraud exists when someone:

- Lies to you except when the lies come from the Government.
- Conceals from you except when the Government does the concealing.
- You justifiably rely on or are hurt by the lie or concealment, an act performed every day by the Government.

If You are Accused of Criminal Fraud:

You can be arrested and convicted of the crime of criminal fraud. Criminal consequences include:

- Imprisonment
- Probation or parole
- Restitution (pay victims for losses)
-

The likelihood of any of the above consequences depends on:

- Severity of the criminal fraud
- Prior convictions
- Attitude of the community and court towards this type of crime
- Currently on probation or parole

You can also be held civilly liable to the victim in a private lawsuit for money. This could include:

- Having a money judgment taken against you
- Punitive damages
- Canceling any contracts

What is Embezzlement?

Embezzlement is the illegal taking of anything (usually money or property), which has been entrusted to that person's care. One example of embezzlement is when an employee entrusted with their employer's money takes it for the employee's own use; embezzlement is a form of White Collar Crime.

Consequences of a Criminal Embezzlement Conviction

- It will be on your record for life
- Imprisonment
- Probation or parole
- Significant fines
- Loss of occupational licensing

What is RICO?

RICO stands for the Federal Racketeer Influenced and Corrupt Organization Act. The act passed by Congress to stop people engaging in a pattern of criminal activity:

- RICO was originally applied to organized crime, as the only way the government could convict mobsters or gangsters
- This is a very complicated area of law that is very vague and ambiguous, so Courts have had to interpret what exactly the act is supposed to mean

What is Racketeering?
- The term racketeering refers generally to a criminal who uses extortion, loan sharking, bribery or obstruction of justice to further their illegal activities
- Usually this person uses some sort of authority or power to illegally persuade others to further his/her interests

Who Can Be Charged with a RICO Violation?
- The person must be employed or associated with a criminal enterprise
- The person's activities must affect interstate commerce
- Just about anything affects interstate commerce! If you use the telephone, internet, railroad, highways, waterways or mail you are using some kind of interstate commerce
- The person charged must have participated with the organization through a pattern or racketeering activity
- The Government looks at whether this persons actions have the same or similar purpose, results, participants, victims and methods
- The statute of limitations (when you can bring a lawsuit) for prosecuting a RICO violation is 5 years for criminal prosecution and 4 years for civil prosecution
- Securities Fraud is any fraud used in connection with the sale of a security
- The law is generally intended to prevent any one from using a scheme to defraud, make untrue statements, or fail to make a statement that deceives investors
- It can also include theft from manipulation of the market, and theft from security accounts
- An investor must rely on information given and they must suffer some type of harm
- The fraud must affect interstate commerce, but this can be as simple as giving information over the telephone or internet

The Prosecution of Securities Fraud
- Civil and administrative actions are brought by the Securities and Exchange Commission (SEC)
- Criminal proceedings are brought by the United States Department of Justice Most states have adopted blue sky laws that are similar to federal laws, so it is possible to be convicted by both the federal and state government for securities fraud. In reality this constitutes Double Jeopardy, illegal under the Constitution!

What Is Tax Evasion?
Tax Evasion is generally defined as any act designed to defraud the IRS. ***This definition is very broad and allows the IRS to come after you for just about any knowing or unknowing misstatements on your taxes.***

When Must the IRS Charge You with Tax Evasion?

Generally you have 6 years for the government to come after you for misstatements on your taxes. But there is no time limit on when the IRS can audit you.

Punishments for Tax Evasion

Punishments for tax evasion can be harsh, including:

- Fines as much as $250,000 for individuals and $500,000 for corporations
- A 75% civil penalty
- Criminal charges, including imprisonment of up to 3 years

Types of Tax Evasion

- **Personal Income Tax evasion**
    - Falsifying income or other factual data
- **Business Tax evasion**
    - Claiming false deductions
    - Deliberately underreporting or omitting income
    - Overstating the amount of deductions
    - Keeping two sets of books, or making false statements in books and records
    - Claiming personal expenses as business expenses
    - Hiding or transferring assets or income
- **Employment Tax Evasion**
    - Failure to pay employment taxes
    - Falsifying payroll
    - Pyramiding
    - Employment leasing
    - Paying employees in case

What are trade secrets?

The Uniform Trade Secret Act defines a trade secret as "information, including a formula, pattern, compilation, program, device, method, technique, or process" that has independent economic value as a result of its secrecy. Trade secrets usually arise in employment settings. There is no need to register a trade secret to get Federal and State Law protections.

Keeping the Trade Secret's Secret

It is getting more and more difficult to maintain the secrecy of a trade secret. In order to maintain the secrecy, employers should develop policies and procedures regarding an employee's use of the trade secret and any communications the employee may make regarding the trade secret.

An employer can address these policies in trainings or orientations as soon as the employee is hired. The employer can also require their employees to sign confidentiality agreements regarding their trade secrets. The employer should clearly convey his or her intent to maintain the
confidentiality of the trade secret.

Of course, the type and scope of crimes that an individual can be charged with are far too many to be outlined here. As noted earlier, most arrests are made against drug users and dealers. Other crimes against individuals and property are less prevalent.

Depending on the charges brought against you it is now that you will decide whether or not or want an attorney to represent you. Of course, it is not necessary for you to hire an attorney now. This decision rest solely with you.

Without an attorney you will be subjected to extensive questioning by the authorities and, unless you have the resolve and fortitude to refuse to answer any and all questions, it is probably wise to ask for one. Either you will contract for your own attorney or, if you cannot afford one and friends or family are not able to afford one, the court will provide a Public Defender to represent your interests.

You will be advised of the charges pending against you during this questioning period. It will do you no good whatsoever to deny any all allegations against you to the authorities. Virtually everyone that they arrest deny their charges and they are totally unsympathetic to you or your denials. Their sole purpose at this point is to continue to build the case against you to be able to formally charge you in a court of law.

Habeas corpus: Latin: "You shall have the body" is a writ, or legal action, through which a person can seek relief from unlawful detention, or the relief of another person. The writ of *habeas corpus* protects persons from harming themselves, or from being harmed by the judicial system. Originally a feature of English law, the writ of *habeas corpus* has historically been an important legal instrument safeguarding individual freedom against arbitrary state action.

A writ of *habeas corpus ad subjiciendum*, also "The Great Writ", is a summons with the force of a court order, addressed to the custodian (e.g. a prison official) demanding that a prisoner be taken before the court, and with proof of authority allowing the court to determine if that custodian has lawful authority to detain the person; if not, the person shall be released from custody. The prisoner, or another person in his or her behalf (e.g. if the prisoner is detained incommunicado), may petition the court, or a judge, for a writ of *habeas corpus ad subjiciendum*.

Notwithstanding, many of those arrested today are considered Detainees and the Government can and does hold "suspects" indefinitely without charges. This is unlawful and unconstitutional but the Government does it anyway!

The "presumption of innocence" is a quaint idea and notion having no basis in law or fact! Vincent Bugliosi, the famous Prosecutor who prosecuted the Manson family and wrote the book HELTER SKELTER, wrote that very same assertion in another book about legal issues and the legal process!

Regardless of what you hear on television from the whole gaggle of police, detective and lawyer shows, **YOU ARE NOT INNOCENT UNTIL PROVEN GUILTY**. The Prosecutor has no such notion. Law enforcement has no such notion. The judge has no such notion. In most instances the jury has no such notion! The mere fact that you were arrested usually gives way to that idea, especially with most juries.

For the most part your arrest will forever change your life. Your family, friends, neighbors and the media will certainly draw their own conclusions about your arrest. Some of those conclusions will never be changed even if all charges are dismissed or you are acquitted by a jury! The stigma of arrest can last a lifetime. Your "alleged" crime will always leave doubt in someone's mind!

In the Federal System, depending on the type and severity of the crime, especially under the Patriot Act, a person is regularly detained without formal charges brought. The Government does not assent to its' own laws. Many citizens are deprived of Due Process since 9/11 under the guise of suspected terrorism. Whether or not you fall into this category will become abundantly clear to you shortly after your arrest.

You will be detained and housed apart from the general population, usually solitary confinement. You will be left alone for days at a time except for meals and showers. You be made to feel that no one is there for you. You will be allowed no visitation, no telephone privileges or contact with others. My advice is to sit it out, attempt to contact the court or an attorney to alleviate your status.

To co-operate or not to co-operate, that is the question. Most people who do not think they have committed a crime, or that the authorities will never prove their charges, believe that by co-operating they will no longer come under law enforcement scrutiny. Maybe, maybe not.

The absolute safe tact to take is to say: **"I have nothing to say"**. Any interrogator will try to convince you that if you have nothing to hide you should have no problem answering their questions.

Do not be lulled into believing that any law enforcement agent has your best interests in mind. They want information, Any information, however innocuous to you, might incriminate you or others in a crime. So stick to: "I have nothing to say".

This may be the most important moment in your arrest and detention process:

Law Enforcement and the Prosecutor, FBI Agents and the U.S. Attorney can lie to you about anything and everything. They can MISREPRESENT the TRUTH. They will attempt to make you believe that they have more information than they really have. They will not be held accountable for any of their statements to you!

If you, however, lie or provide false and misleading statements to any official you will be charged with "obstruction" and any number of other violations that they can conjure. These charges will undoubtedly result in longer sentencing if you are convicted.

WITHIN 3 DAYS OF YOUR ARREST YOU WILL BE ARRAIGNED IN COURT. It is at this hearing that you will be notified of your charge(s), any fines that could be imposed and asked to enter a plea. Guilty, not guilty, Alford or No Contest (Nolo Contendre). If you choose not to enter a plea the Judge will always enter   a Not Guilty plea for you.

The Arraignment is usually a very short event taking mere minutes. The court processes hundreds of these a week in larger cities so the Judges like to keep the traffic moving quickly. It is at this Hearing that bail is requested. Depending on the severity of the accusation the Judge will "set" bail at some amount, generally high enough to make certain that you will return to court for proceedings but not so low that you will renege the money and not show up.

A multi-millionaire is going to have a very high bail depending on the crime. It is perceived that this person has the wherewithal to leave the country, go into hiding or otherwise abscond if he has enough money.

Others may be released on their own recognizance, especially if they have standing in the community and have not committed a heinous or capital crime.

The bail can be paid in a number of ways. Cash or securities for the entire amount is best if you have it. A bail bondsman will charge 10% up front to post bond on your behalf. He will ask for security for the remainder of his exposure of 90%. This can come in the form of a Deed of Trust, Vehicle, Stock, Bonds or anything else of value. **YOU WILL NOT GET YOUR 10% BACK.** If your bail is set high this could very easily amount to thousands of dollars!

Once you are released on bail you will be required to appear in Court when scheduled. You will be notified by the Court or your attorney when those appearances are scheduled. Further, you will not be permitted to leave the jurisdiction without express permission from the U. S. Attorney/Prosecutor while you are free on bail.

If bail is not granted by the Court or if you cannot afford bail, you will be held in a detention facility pending further proceedings.

Chapter 8

YOUR DETENTION

You will be detained in a jail under contract to hold Federal Prisoners or in a Corporation owned and run facility to house Federal Prisoners after you have been charged by the Federal Government.

You may have been held in a city or county jail after your arrest. If both Federal and State charges are pending against you , you may be continue to be housed there until one or the other claims jurisdiction.

These facilities house up to several hundred detained, arrested and convicted individuals. Federal prisoners are usually separated from others by wing, tier, pod, facility, floor or cell. Violent offenders and/or gang members are usually segregated further.

 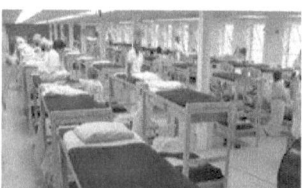

Typical "POD" in a Detention Facility   **Typical "Dorm" in a Detention facility**

After arrest you will be strip and cavity searched, fingerprinted and   photographed as you are processed into the holding facility. You will be required to shower and be issued outer clothing and underwear.

You are not permitted to keep any personal belongings except a wedding ring, eye glasses and an inexpensive religious medallion. The contents of your pockets will be held by the jailers until you are released or transferred. Everything else in your possession must be sent home or donated. This includes all of your clothing and shoes.

You will be interviewed and assessed as to where you will be housed. Those with gang affiliations, gang tattoos and/or prior violent history are usually kept apart from the minor crime or "white collar" accused.

A minimal amount of "hygiene" (toiletries) will be issued: soap, towel, comb, etc.. You will not be allowed to have a razor. A razor will be issued to you each morning so that you can shave and it will be collected within 30 minutes to prevent inmates from fashioning a weapon.

DO NOT SHARE RAZORS!

Hepatitis is more prevalent in prison than anywhere else, especially Hepatitis C. The reason is that it is a blood born disease usually contracted by the sharing of razors, needles (remember, most arrests are for drugs) and tattooing with unclean needles. Tattooing is big in prison even though it is not permitted.

You may be certain that a large number of individuals in prison have Hepatitis in one form or another. Avoid sharing any item (eating utensil, razor, toothbrush, toothpaste, etc.) that will compromise your health. Wash your hands frequently. Clean you sink and toilet frequently.

You will be assigned a bunk or bed of some sort, depending upon the facility. Each cell has one or more bunk beds constructed of steel or cement. A thin mattress will be provided along with a sheet and a blanket

A Cell In The Pod

If there is overcrowding your cell may house others who will sleep on "boats". These are plastic, body length containers with sides that are placed on the floor somewhere within the confines of the already small cell where the other detainee will sleep.

Your cell usually has a toilet and a sink constructed of stainless steel. If you are on lock down you and your cell mates will have virtually no privacy to relieve yourself or clean up.

Showers are located in the common area and shower times are regulated to conserve water and to make certain that all have an opportunity to take a shower.

You will be permitted visitation, telephone, commissary privileges, library or law book access and writing materials. You will be afforded at least one hour per day exercise either in the "yard" or in a gym.

If you are indigent (without funds or family support) you will be given a couple of stamps weekly to mail letters.

You will be given three meals per days usually brought to you and your fellow inmates. These meals meet the minimum requirement for caloric intake, protein and carbohydrates. You may or may not get any fresh fruit or vegetables. Most meals are prepared by inmates supervised by the Correctional staff.

You will be issued a plastic "spork" which is a combination of spoon and fork. You will use this to cut your food, use as a spoon and a fork. Some facilities issue a heavy duty spork which you will use at every meal. Other facilities will issue a lightweight plastic spork each meal which is usually discarded after each meal.

There is a common eating area or dayroom where inmates are fed at the same time in a group. A sugared beverage is usually provided at mealtimes. Coffee will be available in the morning at the breakfast meal. Eating utensils will be made of plastic.

You will usually be required to work at some job in the facility. For this labor you will be "paid" something like $.10 per hour up to $.25 per hour depending on the facility or job that you do. Many are "make work" types of activities to keep you busy: "Idle hands the workshop of the devil" sort of thing!

Many of the jobs are necessary for safety and cleanliness; sweeping, mopping and waxing the common areas and cells. Scrubbing the showers, sinks and toilets. Food Service, cleaning and waxing the hallways. Laundry service. Painting. These tasks will be done as many as three times per day. With your "pay" added to your Commissary account you are able to purchase items such as coffee, candy, pens, paper, envelopes, batteries, radio, sweat clothing, shoes and other food items.

Your account can be replenished by money order from family or friends. Without any funds in your Commissary Account you are left with your three meals per day and no "luxuries" such as a radio, sweats or tennis shoes. There are various ways to "earn" some of these, usually by doing someone else's job for them, ironing their clothing or cleaning their cell. These activities are prohibited but a regularly done by the inmates.

You will be subject to "counts" during the day where the Correction Officers/Jailers regularly do a head count to verify population and that no one has "escaped" or aren't where they are supposed to be. Any count that is "off" results in a "lock-down" where each and every inmate is locked in their cell and another count is taken. If the count is verified then inmates are released to the common area until lights out at night.

Periodically, the jailers will conduct searches, called a "toss", of your area and cells to confiscate any contraband that may have accumulated by the inmates. You will be stripped searched, constrained with handcuffs and situated away from your living area while they conduct a thorough search of every container, mattress, light fixture, ventilation duct, sink, toilet, shower and clothing.

If anything is found that was not issued, or had been modified in any way from its original form it will be confiscated and an incident report will be issued against you or your cell mates. Believe it or not some inmates will "brew" alcoholic beverages, be able to acquire drugs, tobacco, cell phones and other items that seem to be impossible to obtain. Avoid these and those individuals who have them. They can only bring you trouble and compromise your safety and well being.

If the contraband is deemed "dangerous" or consists of drugs or cell phone the inmate(s) will be taken to the Special Housing Unit (SHU), usually solitary/segregation, and be locked down for several weeks with no contact with others except the Correctional Officers. The SHU is sometimes called the "hole".

The Correctional authorities very likely will bring additional charges against the violating inmate resulting in more prison time, if convicted, on top of those charges already pending, .

A disciplinary report against you is called a Shot and will result in a blemish on your file which follows you throughout the jail/prison system. Shots are based upon severity of the infraction, from talking while a count is being taken to rioting or killing. Depending on the severity you will be restricted in your activities to being confined in the SHU or sent to a more secure facility. Again, additional charges can and will be brought against the inmate.

You will be confined with others who constitute the full spectrum of racial makeup, language and culture. Each group will have a "leader" , called a "Shot Caller" who represents that group to others in the cell block or pod. These individuals will act on behalf of their "constituency" on conflicting issues among individuals or groups.

These issues might range from someone disrespecting another, stealing, "buying/selling", "bull dogging" or anything that would never seem an issue anywhere else. Bull dogging is when an inmate or group decides to intimidate you for favors or extortion to share your commissary items or account. The intimidation or threat is real and unless you are allied with another group or are able to thwart these inmates by your own wherewithal you could find yourself co-operating or injured in some way.

The idea is to keep the peace without resorting to violence especially among gang member or gang affiliations. As often as not things will get out of control and confrontations resulting in assault or worse occur, more often than you might think. The Shot Callers can intervene on your behalf so it is wise to make an alliance with the one who can speak on your behalf, if you are in that kind of environment.

While you are in Detention do not, repeat, do not, repeat, do not, repeat, do not discuss your case or your charges with anyone, even your Cellie/Bunkie!

These people are not your friend. After Detention it is unlikely that you ever see them again. It is acceptable to talk about other things with your fellow inmates but do not discuss your case. Everyone has a story. Everyone will tell you the story that puts them in the most favorable light.

Your "story" or case may or may not be used against you. Some people like to embellish their story to make themselves look more favorable, more savvy or more dangerous than they really are. Others can use another's story in an attempt to get a better "deal" for themselves from the Prosecutor or to challenge the other individual's integrity.

Many inmates in Detention and Federal Prison have nothing left but their integrity or what dignity they can muster. They have nothing else to lose. By disrespecting them with a slight, a slur, a disparaging remark heard by others you can be the target of an assault and worse.

Above all, in a confined, incarcerated environment never "dis" (disrespect) a fellow inmate, his family or friends. Keep it to yourself. You will only bring grief from which you have no escape!

If fighting breaks out the jailers will come in force, stop the altercation and place the entire facility on lockdown while they conduct an investigation. This lockdown can last from a day to several weeks, depending on the extent of the violence and injuries sustained during that violence.

Avoid any and all altercations while in Detention! Go to your cell and close the door. It will automatically lock. STAY OUT OF HARMS WAY!

During lockdown, no one leaves their cell, day or night. All food is brought to the cell. There are no telephone privileges, library or exercise.

Never borrow anything from anyone and never lend anything unless you have no expectation of ever seeing it again! No one knows when they are going to be moved, transferred or released. If you have "loaned" someone something you or they may not be around to collect it. On the other hand the individual may simply refuse to return or reimburse you for the item. Is it worth a confrontation? That is a decision you have to make. It is better just not to lend or borrow, period.

Laundry will collected by Trustees, washed and returned once per week.

Medical services will provide the medications that you require after an initial medical exam and assessment shortly after you arrival. You will not be permitted any psychotropic medications.

There will be a "sick call" each morning and evening where you will be issued pills, inhaler for asthmatic conditions, diabetic shots or any other medication for treatment that has been prescribed by the facilities physician. New medical conditions developed after your arrival must be requested and will take some time to address by the medical personnel, sometimes up to several days!

If you have an attorney at this point he will visit you periodically to discuss your case and to advise you on various issues. These are further covered later in this publication. After the Arraignment he should file several Motions with the court.

One will be for Discovery which forces the Prosecutor to reveal any and all information he has regarding your case. This would include Officers and investigators affidavits, interviews with witnesses, time and dates that you were alleged to have committed the crimes they have charged you and any other document the Prosecutor may have.

It is possible that your attorney may file for dismissal, reduction or elimination of bond and other issues affecting your case. You can, of course, perform all of these filing yourself but will not carry the weight to the court of an attorney filed motion.

The Law Library in the Detention Facility gives you opportunities to review the law, various Motions and how to file Briefs supporting your Motions. More often than not there are other inmates who have "worked" the system before and are very familiar with the legal process. They can be very helpful and can perform a lot of preparation for you for a "fee". This fee can range from money being sent to their Commissary account to providing actual commissary items or other "service" such as doing their duties for them, cleaning their cell, etc..

You should be advised that these **"jailhouse lawyers" are only sometimes successful in obtaining anything in the legal process.** Judges often view these filings as frivolous and designed to delay or offer spurious arguments about your case and the charges filed against you. Nonetheless, it may be beneficial to use the Inmate for some of the earlier filings that are commonly done.

Formal communication with jail officials are accomplished with what are called "cop outs' or "kites". These are used to address grievances, seek permission for various issues and to request special medical treatment or medications. Response is usually slow and require multiple submissions to higher authority within the jail chain of command to get results.

Periodically you will be required to appear before the court as your case proceeds. This can be done by video conferencing on simple rulings over motions or you may be transported to the court for more formal proceedings. You will be shackled, hands and feet and appear before the Judge in your jail uniform.

All this is designed to demean and degrade you in the courtroom. You look like a criminal, you look like you are guilty and you look like you need to be sentenced for a very long time by the

Judge.

Unless you are being tried before a jury (and sometimes even then) you will always wear jail clothing and be shackled while in the courtroom.

When all is said and done, if you are released for lack of evidence or the investigation has resulted in another being arrested for your "crime" or even bring acquitted by a jury, the fact remains that you have lost your freedom for however long you were in jail. There will be no apology, no compensation for lost wages or for "false imprisonment". You are on your own.

You have no recourse but to pick up the pieces of your life and make an attempt to get a normal life back. The Government is uncaring, insensitive and aloof to you or your well being.

Chapter 9

Jurisdiction
("Straw Man", "Actors", "Players")

Remember, this guideline is directed to those of you who have come under Federal investigation, indictment or arrest. You are in the Federal jurisdiction. State jurisdictions often process crimes and criminals in similar fashion to the "Feds" . Often, they will "share" crimes and criminals to maximize penalties and media coverage.

If, for example, multiple charges are brought by local authorities against an individual it is not uncommon for the State to prosecute some of those charges and the Feds to prosecute others! Sometimes this is called selective prosecution and, in it's purest form is illegal and unethical. However, the States and Feds do this regularly in the spirit of co-operation. In this way your double jeopardy rights can be circumvented because they are brought under different jurisdictions!

There are other ways that a jurisdiction can violate the sanctity of double jeopardy simply by applying the sub-title of a particular of a criminal code or using a similar law but incorporating different verbiage! The clever bastards will do anything to obtain a conviction whether it violates law, ethics or conscience!

You must be vigilant and do everything possible to familiarize yourself with the laws affecting your charges. That is why you hire a lawyer but you   must be particularly vigilant with him. It is your freedom at stake, not his. It is your money that you pay for every moment of time he spends even thinking about your case. Your entire life is forever changed as a result of Criminal charges brought against you by the Federal Government.

You must take an active part in your defense, whether your lawyer likes it or not!

There are 90 Federal District Courts in the 50 States. There are 90 U.S. Attorney's serving those District Courts who prosecute Criminal , Civil and Debt Charges. Each U.S. Attorney has at least five Assistant U.S. Attorney's or Prosecutors who do the actual work of processing you through the SYSTEM. The total number is over 5,000 in the United States. They are very, very busy because there is no end to the criminals that are Indicted or arrested.

To protect these Judges and Prosecutors the United States Marshals service is employed. Their duties include transportation of Federal prisoners in custody, acting as bailiff in the Federal Courtrooms, "body guard" to Judges and Prosecutors after hours and apprehending suspects who have outstanding warrants, have escape or absconded from low level security facilities such as half-way houses and home confinement.

You will be prosecuted under one or more of some 3,200 Federal Judges who are appointed for life on the various courts (2,650 District Court Judges, 687 Appellate Court Judges, 50 Circuit Court Judges).

The United States Government should be operating under the Uniform Commercial Code yet, over time, the Corporation of the United States of America has infringed upon the property, rights and life of its' citizens and States without opposition. Most derive some benefit from the Federal Government and it is easier to lick the boot of your benefactor than to endure the wrath of penalties that the Government will impose.

The Corporation of the United States of America, through charade and a number of other subterfuges brings Criminal and Statutory Criminal charges against more than a quarter of a million citizens each and every year! These are bought through Federal Grand Jury indictments, Arrests made by the Federal Bureau of Investigation, The Drug Enforcement Administration (DEA), The Food and Drug Administration (FDA), The Department of Treasury (Alcohol, Tobacco, Firearms and Explosives {ATF}) and a whole plethora of other agencies including local law enforcement.

The U.S.A. Corporation makes "high theater" by claiming that they have the authority and power to circumvent their own laws to arrest and Prosecute its' citizens. By virtue of the fact that they do this every day gives credence to their nefarious acts. Remember, any act or statement left unchallenged or unopposed becomes fact under law!

The government has to bring you into it's Jurisdiction by making you a "STRAW MAN" or a substitute for your real persona. When you receive your indictment or a list of charges brought against you, your name will be in all capital letters. By this seemingly innocuous act the government, in effect, has made you a Criminal under the Uniform Commercial Code, a farce.

As a defendant in any Criminal Case you are changed legally into a "STRAW MAN" so that the court has jurisdiction over you. This, of course, is not evident to you because your lawyer deems it not necessary to inform you of this fact and the court certainly will not so as to add a "complication" to their expeditious proceedings against you!

Each and every participant in your "crime" and in the courtroom is an "ACTOR" furthering the charade of legitimacy in the proceedings. These are legal terms that are clearly defined in Blacks Law Dictionary but rarely used in the courtroom except to make legal points in arguments through briefs or motions.

It is by this and the fact that you will present yourself to the Court for Arraignment in front of the "Bar" (the low railing separating the gallery from the court itself) that you place yourself under the jurisdiction of the court. Otherwise, a legal argument could be made, although not very successfully in the past, that the Federal Court has no jurisdiction over you unless you committed your crime in the District of Columbia in Washington.

As you place yourself under the Jurisdiction of the court (or they slyly do it for you) everyone involved in the proceedings from then on are "players" in the "high theater" of the process.

Think about a tomato canning plant putting tomatoes into cans on a mechanized assembly line. You are going to be "processed" like so may tomatoes going from one place to another, ultimately being "canned" if they have their way! And throughout this entire process you are going to be given the impression that every effort is being made to assure a fair and proper defense and/or trial, while the "PLAYERS" in the court work the system to assure that every advantage is on their side to make certain that you are "canned"!

Confused? So are 99% of all other Americans. This is something your lawyer probably won't want to comment on.

Further, if you persist with your lawyer in trying to take a Uniform Commercial Code   tact to press for a dismissal he will likely advise against it or charge you exorbitant fees to prepare the necessary documents to present to the court. The court will likely reject this argument anyway even though there is legal precedent in your favor, however ambiguous.

- *There is one avenue that you, as an arrested individual , **may** be able to do at your Arraignment to bring about an immediate dismissal.*

  In the Uniform Commercial Code there is a clause 27CFR §72.11 with which by simply ignoring your name when Arraigned, not taking any oath and stating to the Judge "Do you hold the bond on this issue"? ; might, just might result in an immediate dismissal because the Court does not hold the bond. Again, consult an Attorney for legal advise regarding these obscure issues. He, for certain, has no clue regarding the UCC in a Criminal Case and will advise against any pursuit of such a action!

This is not something that you will read in the Constitution, learn in Civics or Government classes as you go through academia.

Many have tried to file themselves under the   UCC 1 (Uniform Commercial Code)   to remove themselves from the jurisdiction of the Federal Government for criminal offenses, however, these have not been successful once these charges have been already filed against the individual.

You are revenue to the United States Government which begs, borrows and steals all the money it can to keep afloat and its citizen mollified.

The trillions of dollars reported regularly as the "national debt" is but a drop in the bucket to the real debt owed by the United States. It will never be paid but may be "forgiven" as we move to a State of Communism which has been insipidly creeping over us each year.

The bottom line is that the Court will claim and have jurisdiction over you, whether you are brought before a Local, State or Federal Court. You may be shuffled from Judge to Judge as you move the "Process" of Arraignments, Hearings, Motions and Sentencing's. They are all acting in concert with the intent to "Process" you as quickly and efficiently as possible. After all, there are hundreds, if not thousands awaiting with you and coming into the "System" to be processed also.

There are only so many Judges, so many courtrooms and only so much time to handle the traffic! If you do anything to impede this "Process" , especially by demanding a trial, you are going to receive extra special attention which will manifest itself in your length of sentence should you be found guilty!

After the Courts are finished with you, you will move from one jurisdiction to another. From the Federal Criminal Justice Court, to the Bureau of Prisons (BOP) to Probation.

Chapter 10

The Prosecutor: your worst enemy!

- *The Federal Criminal Justice System is never about finding TRUTH.*
- *It is what the Prosecutor can or cannot prove in a Court of Law!*

He will use every tool available to win his case and has no qualms whatsoever about using you to further his career by convicting you and seeing that you go to prison.

If he is later to be found wrong he will never apologize and will blithely continue to prosecute any and all to keep he win record intact.

Fewer than 3% of all Indictments are tried in Court with a jury! More on that later.

The primary reason that Federal Prosecutors have a 97% conviction rate is that they and their Law Enforcement buddies "stack" so many charges against you that you are virtually compelled to accept a plea offer of guilty to one or more "lesser" charges so that you don't spend a large portion of your life in prison!

This, after you have spent a sizable portion of your savings or equity in your home in an attempt to defend yourself.

The Prosecutor is an expert in courtroom maneuvering and legal wrangling. He spends infinitely more time Prosecuting than any Defense attorney spends defending. The Prosecutor is familiar with Judges pet peeves and quirks. He is on familiar ground and is a wily, clever and unscrupulous adversary. Beware of this evil person.

Here is how the clever bastards work.............

After an arrest with obvious evidence collected such as drugs, firearms, paraphernalia, stolen property, fingerprints at a scene, recorded conversations, observation by Law Enforcement or any other means.................or..............
if you have been under investigation for some period of time, the Assistant U.S. Attorney in the District where your alleged "crime" was committed.................or..............
the District where you now reside or were apprehended will bring those charges to a Grand Jury.

When the AUSA brings the charges to a Grand Jury to bring back a "Bill" he will always have more charges to present than the simple Crime you are alleged to have committed.

For example: Returning to the Drug "Crimes" that 70% of all arrestees face......

If the arresting officer finds a pipe with traces of crack cocaine in the pipe you will first be charged with crack cocaine possession.

- *A paraphernalia charge will be added.*

- *Conspiracy or co-conspiracy will be added once an investigation has revealed that your so-called "friends" have helped them to determine that you are a regular user and maybe even sold some.*

- *A charge of Intent to Distribute will be added and so it goes.*

You will be informed at your Arraignment by the Prosecutor (Assistant U.S. Attorney) that these combined charges will bring you X number of years in prison (a long time!) and upwards of a $250,000.00+ fine if convicted.

Initially, you will plea "Not Guilty" and the "dance" will begin. Your attorney will file a number of motions and briefs in the expectation that your charges will be reduced or that you will win a dismissal before the real "dance" begins. These are not usually successful.

As the Prosecutor continues his investigation more charges may be "stacked" and brought against you. Over the last twenty years Federal Agents and prosecutors have broken the law hundreds of times in their pursuit of justice. They lied, hid evidence, distorted facts, engaged in cover-ups, paid for perjury and set up innocent people in a relentless effort to win indictments, guilty pleas and convictions.

"Victims of Government misconduct sometimes lost their jobs, assets and even their families. Some remain in prison because Federal Prosecutors withheld favorable evidence or allowed fabricated testimony sometimes made by paid informants. '

Some criminals walk free as a reward for conspiring with the Government to deny the rights of others! Promises of lenient sentences and huge Government checks encourage criminals to lie on the witness stand. Inmates in Federal prison sometimes barter or buy information that only an insider to a crime could know sometimes with officials with access to federal crime files. '

They, then memorize these files and get others to do the same. They are able to bargain for reduced sentences by "informing" about crimes by people they have never met in places they have never been. This scam only succeeds because of the tacit approval of law enforcement officers including the FBI!"

A person who fights a federal charge must, by law, receive more prison time than someone who pleads guilty to the same crime. The courts will punish you for tying up the Court when hundreds of other actions can be processed in the same amount of time as a trial!

The courts and the judge used to be a buffer between Prosecutors and the rights of the defendant. Now they are both a rubber stamp for the Prosecutor in the interest of expediency!

- ## The Government has absolute immunity from any wrongdoing in a criminal trial!

Prosecutors generally "taint" the jury pool and arouse public outrage by leaking sometimes false information to the media. The Prosecutor has but one objective and Truth and Justice are not in that equation. They are there to convict, either by plea or by a jury. They care nothing about you. You are another statistic that is going to make his career, period!

At trial the Prosecutors frame their questions, not to get to the truth or seek justice, but to assure that the response will be favorable to the Prosecutors case! Any elaboration by the person testifying to clarify his answer or to direct the answer towards the truth will be met with an admonishment by the Prosecutor and the Judge. The witness will not be permitted to fully express the true facts or truth regarding the case!

You will be asked whether you want to waive your right to speedy trial. Without a waiver you could go to trial in as short a time as 31 days. Without a waiver the Government must try you within 70 days of your Arraignment.

The question of speedy trial is one that plays a strategic role in your defense. Whether you are in or out of jail awaiting disposition of your case plays some role in your decision to waive speedy trail, especially if you are reasonable certain that the Government will win a conviction against you.

The Federal Government does not care that you had no knowledge that your act was a criminal act, no matter what law was violated. The Latin term is called *Mens Rea* ("guilty mind") According to Blacks Law Dictionary, the lexicon of the legal profession, mens rea is the second of two essential elements of every crime at common law., the other being *actus reus*- also termed as a mental element......**criminal intent, guilty mind**!

- *There are only two states of mind which constitutes mens rea, and they are intention and recklessness.*

- *Criminal Intent: An intent to commit an actus reus (wrongful deed or forbidden act to establish criminal liability- a crime constituted by an event)*

- *Double Jeopardy is alive and well in the Judicial process even though it is unconstitutional! The Prosecutor can bring the same or similar charge under different language or Criminal Code to circumvent the Double Jeopardy Law. Further, by "selective prosecution agreement between the Federal Government and State Government, each separate Jurisdictions, double jeopardy can be circumvented! Under the newly enacted "Blue Laws" certain crimes can be tried twice by a Prosecutor!*

- *If your attorney wins a dismissal for you or the judge dismisses for lack of evidence the Prosecution can bring the same and more charges against you within seven years. It is imperative that your lawyer insist upon a Dismissal WITH PREJUDICE from the judge so that the Prosecutor cannot recharge you for the same crime.*

- *Deal or No Deal? Be very careful of any "deal" offered by the Prosecution. Unless the deal is carefully structured you could very well spend more time incarcerated than you were led to believe.*

All Prosecutors are evil, capricious, vindictive and rotten to the core. They derive sadistic pleasure in your conviction and gloat over your prison term sentence!

Any assertion made in court is taken as fact unless challenged by the opposing attorney by "objection". It is by this omission by opposing attorney (usually the defense attorney) that the Prosecutor brings spurious or false allegations into the Court before the judge or jury which, later, are looked at by the Appellate Court. Because no objection was mounted by our attorney, any later argument about the veracity of allegation on appeal will not be considered by the upper court.

Your attorney must carefully weigh every statement made by every witness or piece of evidence introduced by the Prosecutor and mount the objection, even to the extent of trying the patience of the judge. Remember, it is your freedom at stake here, not theirs! If you believe that an objection needs to be made during the proceeding you must impose upon your attorney to make that objection, if he hasn't already.

Chapter 11

Evidence, Affidavits, Discovery

Evidence can come in many forms:

Tangible evidence is, of course, the easiest to determine;   Drugs found at arrest, in a residence or vehicle. A firearm. Documents. Telephone, Fax and Email records. Bank account activity. Caught in the commission of a crime. Video and photos. Recordings from personal contact, wiretaps and other conversations. The list is unending. Tangible evidence is the most difficult to disprove or dispute because it is real, easily seen and compelling.

DNA can be the irrefutable evidence that you were involved in some sort of crime. DNA can be derived from hair, perspiration, tears, sperm, blood, skin, saliva, urine and even feces. Until a couple of years ago it took many weeks to map the DNA of anything taken at a crime scene or placing a suspect at some location. Moreover, there wasn't a sizable data base with which to compare DNA. Law Enforcement had to find a suspect, obtain a warrant to get a DNA sample and wait several weeks for the results.

Today, DNA results can be mapped in a matter of hours and the DNA data pool is substantial. By law every person convicted of a felony must submit to a DNA test. This data is stored in a Law Enforcement Nationwide Computer data base and can be compared in a matter of minutes to any sample taken at a crime scene. When such evidence is presented in Court against an accused suspect, if the DNA matches the accused, the Prosecutor has all but won his case.

Intangible evidence is more ambiguous and sometimes called circumstantial evidence. It can be hearsay or accusations of a third party who was not privy to an actual conversation or witness to a criminal act. Alibi's while a crime was committed are often circumstantial unless the person(s) substantiating the alibi are credible or the alibi is irrefutable.

A vehicle, firearm or clothing seen or used in the commission of a crime but no actual witness of the individual owning those items can be circumstantial evidence. Ballistics from a firearm can be tangible if the firearm is already in evidence or circumstantial if the firearm was never identified or found.

Evidence may be brought to a Grand Jury or the court by the Prosecutor to obtain a "bill" from the Grand Jury and/or obtain an arrest warrant from the judge. However, when at trial all evidence must be introduced only after laying foundation for how and where the evidence was gathered or found. This is usually accomplished by interrogating an officer of the law or a witness who actually confiscated the evidence. How the evidence was handled after during and after arrest   or exercising a search warrant plays a very important part in the integrity of the evidence introduced.

"Chain of Custody"   must be meticulously maintained to assure that the evidence, whatever it may be, has not been tainted in any way. Drugs disappearing or increased in volume from time of confiscation until introduction at trial has "tainted" this evidence.

Money's that might have been secured, missing documents or financial statements and any number of other possibilities must be considered. Evidence is often handled by more than one person after taken by authorities. It is imperative that a scrupulous record of who handled what when be maintained to ensure the integrity of any evidence gathered at the time of arrest and subsequent searches. It must be held in a secure area for sometimes up to several years as the accused winds his way through the Criminal Injustice System.

Affidavits are sworn statements written under oath by law enforcement agents and sometimes witnesses as to facts surrounding an arrest or written allocution by the witness regarding the alleged crime. An affidavit is brought before the Grand Jury or judge and becomes part of the record of the case. It is a crime to make false or misleading statements in an affidavit. An affidavit is sometimes used in lieu of having to present oneself before the court or jury.

You or your lawyer must carefully read any and all affidavits surrounding your arrest. *Read it carefully and over and over again.* *Your lawyer was not there at your arrest so he will not be aware of any false or misleading statements in the affidavit!*

Make notes on anything you see anything that is not correct or subject to interpretation. You must challenge any and all inaccuracies or misrepresentations in affidavits submitted by law enforcement. You can do this with motions and by interrogation at trial. You will need every scrap of legal wrangling to mount an effective defense against accusations brought by the Federal Government against you!

Always remember: Any statement or allegation left unchallenged by you in or out of court becomes a FACT, whether it is true or not! You will NOT be able to use any issue for appeal unless it was challenged (objected to) at your hearings or trial.

Discovery: After you are arrested and have been charged with a crime, copies of any and all documents related to the Prosecutors investigation must be provided to you or your attorney. These include affidavits, interviews with witnesses, a list of witnesses, videos, recordings, photos and everything else that may reside in the Prosecutors files or could be considered as evidence.

Prosecutors regularly withhold some items in the hopes and expectation that they can become bargaining tools to negotiate a plea or bring to trial without sufficient time for you or your attorney to gather refuting testimony or evidence.

Again, every item obtained during Discovery must be carefully reviewed as to veracity and content. It may be that the evidence against you is so overwhelming that a plea might be your only hope of a reduced sentence. The question then becomes....how quickly do you want to negotiate for the plea? Are you out on bond? If you are held without bond or cannot pay for bond and are in detention you may want to move quickly to reduce your overall time in confinement. These considerations must be weighed against any other options available to you.

Chapter 12

Lawyers and Lawyering
$$$Ka-Ching, Ka-Ching$$$©

First of all, you must understand that the laws Congress passes, Law Enforcement makes arrests under, Prosecutors prosecute and that Judges sentence the guilty are <u>all</u> designed and processed by lawyers! Remember, more than 25,000,000 laws on the books and 10,000,000 arrests each and every year!

The "Priesthood of Lawyers" performs before hallowed symbols. The elevated HIGH PRIEST JUDGES platform, the flag, the judge in the robe of a HIGH PRIEST, the gavel, the water pitcher, the reporters recording the proceedings and the clerks making notations in the calendar and computers.

They "chant" in a dead language (Latin) from time to time and, indeed, have a language unto themselves (legalese). It virtually impossible for John Q. Citizen to navigate that process without the aid of an attorney.

A Modern Courtroom   **"Throne" of the HIGH PRIEST JUDGE**

Whoever is the   most persuasive in the courtroom is the winner! Truth be damned. Justice be damned. Innocence or guilt be damned.

"RESULT" is the conclusion of a lawyers work on their clients behalf. The "RESULT" may be a dismissal, an acquittal or a conviction, by plea or jury verdict, it is all the same.

If you understand nothing as you sort through all of this you must understand these facts:

- *The Lawyers foremost obligation is to the United States Government to which he owes his livelihood to Practice law.*

- *The Lawyers second obligation is to the Court itself where he regularly plies his trade at the behest of the Court.*

- *The Lawyers last and final obligation is to you, the defendant, who falls far short of his first two obligations to the Government and the Court!*

TO HAVE A GOOD LAWYER

Your lawyer is interested in defending you to the extent that you are willing to pay. He will extract his fees before he does one iota of work on   your   behalf.

We hope to mitigate those fees by providing you with ammunition with which to negotiate and to make an intelligent decision on how to proceed with your defense. You are well advised to make every effort to know about the laws affecting your arrest as well as those cases which have been
adjudicated in the past and their outcome.

Your lawyer can and will charge you <u>by the minute </u> to do this research using associates, clerks, paralegals and investigators.

$$$Ka-Ching, Ka-Ching$$$©

Every phone call by you or he, every letter generated that must be read, every trip to and from visiting you, every conversation you or he has with you, your family, a witness, a person of interest ……….

Every motion, brief, consult, subpoena, memo, note, document reviewed, character references solicited and more will result in an itemized fee for that service. If your lawyer is reading, thinking, talking and traveling he will bill you for his services.

Court appearances and waiting for your case to be called on the Docket are always billed at higher rates!

Often he will not even look at your case/folder after hired until the day or minute you visit or call him or he visits you in detention, county jail or prison.

Even the lawyer that you may eventually hire may not know anything about the law under which your charges have been brought. You will be paying him to research your charges and Shepherding the law to mount a defense before he can even start to help you.

"Shepherding" is the method lawyers use to work through the maze of rulings, precedents and arguments used in like cases over decades. These routings are spelled out in the SHEPHERDING Legal Book.

You should be very specific when you ask your lawyer about your charges and listen carefully to his response. His ability to aggressively represent you is paramount to a dismissal, minimal sentence or other consideration which will both save you money and potential time in prison!

In essence, the law can mean anything the Prosecutor and the Court wants it to mean, always in their favor. The courts do not want you playing in their "game" and have implemented every sort of subterfuge and stumbling block to deter you from defending yourself. You have probably heard that only a fool will defend himself in a Court of Law. In fact, most Lawyers will not even defend themselves if they are a "defendant".

However, you can do much for yourself before you hire a lawyer, especially through the first stages of the process, i.e., Arraignment, petitioning for bail, filing for dismissals, asking for discovery, etc. . This is not legal advice but merely providing information that you may find useful.

Unfortunately, most people arrested do not have the time, resources or wherewithal to ferret out the necessary information to help your own case. The Internet is extremely useful in today's world. Most State and Federal Laws and remedies are readily available if you conduct the proper searches. Most inmates do not have any access to computers while detained so this is a problem.

There is money in complexity and the Governments Criminal Justice System is as Complex as any in America. Well, maybe not quite. One only has to look at the more than 25,000 pages of the Internal Revenue Service Tax Code gobbledygook that no two IRS agents can agree upon to know how the United States Government conspires to defeat you legally at every front.

$$$Ka-Ching, Ka-Ching$$$©

There are 190 United States Colleges and Universities that graduate more than 30,000 Lawyers each and every year. The Legal SYSTEM must continue to be expanded and become more complicated to assure that these hoard of lawyers have meaningful employment.

Japan has half the population of the United States and the entire nation has less than 100,000 lawyers! Japans incarceration rate is less than 10% of the United States incarceration rate!

The United States has 1,500,000 lawyers and they all have to eat, buy homes, drive nice cars and, if they are Class Action Lawsuitors, must have a Gulf Stream 5 personal jet as a status symbol!

Granted, most lawyers opt for Corporate Law or Banking to go after the big bucks. Civil lawyers abound but Criminal Lawyers are a special breed to themselves.

We all have seen the Lawyer "shows" on TV and how criminal lawyers work their clients and the system. All very entertaining but less based on the real world than on a one hour venue which every case opens and closes. Those shows compress into one hour than often takes years to bring to any sort of conclusion, even with a straight guilty plea.

During that time your lawyer is "working" your case, seemingly every day!

- ## You only represent billable hours to a lawyer!

$$$Ka-Ching, Ka-Ching$$$©

Your lawyer will smile, act like he is worrying for you, exude confidence in his ability to defend you and he will lull you into believing that he is your salvation, that he will win a dismissal or acquittal or mount the most aggressive defense found anywhere.

- ## Win, lose or mistrial your lawyer will get paid, in advance!

Lawyers are the only profession that receives payment with no recourse if you do not receive a favorable result! A Doctor can be sued for malpractice. A Mechanics Lean on your property can be removed and the Contractor sued for faulty workmanship. But your lawyer, your lawyer is virtually immune from any liability due to malfeasance or incompetence, thanks to the laws that they designed for themselves and their relationship with judges who are always lawyers first!

$$$Ka-Ching, Ka-Ching$$$©

You will pay a retainer in advance and receive itemized statements on a not-so-regular basis. As your retainer depletes your lawyer will ask you for more money, in advance. You will astonished at the line item billings. Some will be indecipherable and will be explained with guile and conviction. You will easily get the impression that you must be only client that your attorney has because every single waking hour seems to be billed to you.

In your lawyers defense you should realize that he is not the only person working on your case. Often, to mitigate costs, he will have paralegals, clerks and secretaries research and write Briefs, Motions and other filings. Much of this is "boil plate" or already on file. He may also have to hire investigators to interview witnesses and other individuals to properly mount your defense.

Regardless, what ever you think that your defense will cost, or what your lawyer tells you it will cost, it is not unreasonable to double it and add some! Win, lose or mistrial!

Oh, their argument is that you can file a 2255 remedy **for ineffective counsel (incompetent representation!)** if you were to lose your case. They won't tell you this up front though and you will generally learn about this remedy after you are incarcerated! That sounds well and good but the fact is, once you win that argument (if you do), you must start the process all over again with another lawyer, more time, more money!

$$$Ka-Ching, Ka-Ching$$$©

When you go to court on a hearing, motion or trial your attorney must carefully weigh every statement made by every witness or piece of evidence introduced by the Prosecutor and mount an objection where warranted, even to the extent of trying the patience of the judge. Often witnesses will make statements lead by the Prosecutor which are false, misleading or irrelevant. Remember, it is your freedom at stake here, not theirs! If you believe that an objection needs to be made during the proceeding you must impose upon your attorney to make that objection, if he hasn't already.

Chapter 13

Questions to ask your Lawyer

- *How long have you been "practicing" Criminal Law?   (This goes to experience?)*

- *Were you ever a Prosecutor? If so, why did you change to a Defense Lawyer?*
  (Either works for or against you depending on his notion of real "justice")

- *How many cases have you defended?   (Courtroom experience)*

- *Referrals?   (Beware if none)*

- *How many cases similar to mine have you defended.*
  (Experience and familiarity with legal aspects that can reduce research costs)

- *What is your "Win" vs. "Lose" record? (good luck getting a straight answer on this!)*
  (How good is this guy?)

- *How many cases have you "plead out" versus "Dismissals"?*
  (Cases a lost cause or does it show good legal representative)

- *How many cases have you plead out versus going to trial.*
  (Lost cause or "churning money from you"..v.. a good defensive case)

- *What is your relationship with the U.S. Attorney/Prosecutor? Socially? Professionally?*
  (If all buddies beware!)

- *What is your relationship with the Judge? Socially? Professionally?*
  (No lawyer will jeopardize his relationship with a Judge)

- *What do know know about the Uniform Commercial Code?   (Nearly always, nothing)*

- *Have you used the UCC in a Criminal Defense? Result?   (Probably never!)*

- *If not, why not?   (Considers it futile or spurious)*

- *How much is your retainer? Will you take security other than cash?*
  (Bread and butter for him- will not start anything without this)

- *What is your hourly fee? How often do you bill? Itemized statement?*
  (Expect high fees for Federal charges, i.e., > $250.00 per hour)

- *Will you cap the fee for my defense? My maximum financial exposure?*
  (Probably not, ever. If you lose he will work you for the Appeal process for even more money)

Chapter 14

The $$$Ka-Ching, Ka-Ching$$$© Factor

As noted throughout this little treatise you will notice the **$$$Ka-Ching, Ka-Ching$$$©** along the way. You will see it further on also. The reasons are obvious.

Aside from the costs which you will incur from legal services, bail that you yourself put up or a bondsman put up for you, you may suffer financial loss from potential loss of job or other income.

These take a huge toll over the time it takes to navigate the Criminal Justice ("InJustice") System. In order to defend yourself from the allegations made by the Federal Government you may have to sell or mortgage your real estate holdings or sell stock or other securities. You may even have to sell personal property such as vehicles, jewelry or anything else of value that you possess.

Of course, this depends upon whether or not the Government has seized your assets no longer allowing you to use them to fund your defense or to support you or your family through the ordeal.

And the ordeal can be long and tedious. It will affect you, your family and place them in a precarious financial situation, especially if you are not able to provide any sort of income.

The United States Government has unlimited time and resources with which to mount a case against you. They have the manpower and data base to investigate every aspect of your life. The Government can trace virtually your entire life back to your birth.

They can and will interview many "witnesses" and use every ploy in an attempt to groom informants (snitches) to testify against you. A witness brings much more to the "party" than physical evidence.

And all the while you are paying your attorney to review every piece of paper brought to him through Discovery and his own effort on your behalf. The costs will mount dramatically as time goes on!

If your resources are such that you do not have the wherewithal to pay for legal services you will be given a Federal Public Defender to represent your interests to the Court.

The Public Defender will not cost you anything. He is paid by the Government (taxpayer) to represent you against charges and allegations made by the Government against you!

In any event, your legal wrangling through the Federal Criminal InJustice System is going to take from several months to several years. Your life is essentially on hold while you are going through the "good news", "bad news" cycles that prevail over that time! You can never be certain of the outcome, even with the best lawyers and spending a fortune in fees!

Chapter 15

Your Public Defender (aka "Public Pretender")

If your resources are such that you do not have the wherewithal to pay for legal services you will be given a Federal Public Defender to represent your interests to the Court.

Those who might have used a Public Defender in the past often call them "Public Pretenders". While this is a slur on their record of regularly pleading out their clients and offering a not-so-vigorous defense on you behalf they do provide a modicum of representation for you.

Your Public Defender costs you nothing and they do a reasonable job of navigating the Criminal Justice System. They are , however, heavily burdened with cases and cannot allocate a lot of time or resources to your particular case!

Remember, you always get what you pay for!

Because of case load the Government often contracts with outside Law firms to represent you. You will get a slightly better defense representation with one of these contract lawyers than a Federal Public Defender.

In either instance their case loads are always monumental and they are not able to spend much time on your case. It is not unusual for your Public Defender to have 200 or more cases assigned to him. It is his intention to "plea you out" as often as possible. He does not have the time or wherewithal to be your trial lawyer!

Often they will not even look at your file until the day that you and he have some communication, in person or by telephone.

His file is updated by his clerk or secretary as data and information is received by his office. Before your case ever gets to the plea stage or trial the file will become quite thick with Discovery, Interrogatories, Indictment, Charges, Motions, Briefs and Rebuttals.

Of course, he will attend each and every Court hearing on your behalf, with or without you. This, itself, consumes much of the Public Defenders time, especially with the number of cases assigned to him. To do the proper and extensive work to mount an effective defense for you or anyone else is beyond the capability of he or his staff. Therefore, he is nearly compelled to work with the Prosecutor to Plea your case to lesser charges.

Chapter 16
YOUR RIGHTS
You have some left!

- You always have the right to an attorney, should you desire one. Even if you can't afford an attorney the Courts will assign a Federal Public Defender to represent you. Your Public Defender is assigned from a pool of Federal Public Defenders who are assigned in any jurisdiction. He will consult with you regularly and inform you of pending hearings and always be with you when interviewed by Law Enforcement, the prosecutors or the court (judge).

- You have the right to defend yourself and to avail yourself of any and all legal books and documents with which to do so. You can petition the Court with motions and briefs and obtain any and all documents that your lawyer has access to through Discovery.

- You are not required to speak to anyone about anything, especially Law Enforcement or a Prosecutor, with or without an attorney. Without an attorney, however, interrogations can be lengthy and you can be held without a formal arrest for several days.

- You have the option of demanding a speedy trial or waive this right which will delay proceedings, sometimes indefinitely.

- You can accept or reject any plea offered by the Prosecution and even counter-offer his plea. He will usually offer a plea which reduces some of the charges in the expectation that you will accept the lesser charge(s) rather than go to trial. He may or may not accept any counter-offer depending on how badly he wants to convict you to improve his own reputation and status.

- You can confront any witness the Prosecution brings to testify against you at trial.

- You are entitled to any and all evidence against you through the Discovery process.

- The Government must provide medical care while you are detained or incarcerated.

- Meals must be provided each day you are detained, transported or incarcerated.

- "Hygiene", i.e., soap, toothpaste, toothbrush and towel must be provided to you.

- Writing materials and telephone privileges must be provided unless you have committed an infraction while detained or incarcerated. Sometimes privileges can be rescinded for up to 6 months depending upon the severity of the infraction.

- You can ask for a Change of Venue because of the media coverage of your charge, your celebrity, and/or your arrest because you would not get a jury pool without pre-conceived notions of your crime. Judges hate to rule for Change of Venue because of increased costs and other factors. He will usually rule that any possible jury tainting by the media can be overcome by voir dire (question of the jurors during jury selection).

- You are not required to testify at your trial. In fact, it is usually a detriment to your case if you do. The Prosecutor is a skilled interrogator and will ask questions on cross examination that will require you to answer in such a way to favor his case, not yours!

Chapter 17

The "Process"
Lots of $$$Ka-Ching, Ka-Ching$$$© !

After your arrest you will try to get **bail** set in an amount that you can afford. You or your attorney can do this at your Arraignment. All Arraignments must be held by the Court within 72 hours of your arrest unless you are being "detained" by Federal Authorities.

The **booking** process was covered earlier in this publication.

You will be Arraigned where the formal charges will be specified as well as any fines that are applicable. At the arraignment you will enter a plea. The amount of bail will be set at this time.

You will either "bail out" or not depending upon your financial situation. If not, you will be held in a Detention facility which could be a County Jail, City Jail or other contracted facility such as a CCA (Corrections Corporation of America). You will be housed there in a unit which will have a number of other accused, those awaiting transportation after conviction

Your detainment can be an indeterminate period of time but generally less with an attorney. The Court must offer reasonable bail in accordance with your Bill of Rights but can also impose a prohibitively high bail of you are a flight risk or are extremely wealthy. Murderers and other heinous criminals such as terrorism will not be allowed bail to assure that the crime will be prosecuted.

Depending on the media attention that your arrest draws you will be subject to many changes in your life. Financially, you will begin to draw down your bank accounts to defend against the allegations brought by the Government.

Personally, you will find yourself in a higher state of stress as the full import of what you are facing begins to register.

You will see a change in attitude among family member and friends. Your business associates will be either supportive or aloof but there will be a significant change in how they interact with you. If you are out on bail and able to continue your job count this as a blessing.

Many accused by the Government are terminated by their employer depriving them of income needed to support himself, his family and pay the ever mounting legal fees.

The Process through the Federal Criminal Justice System can take years. During this time you or your Lawyer will be conducting the "DANCE" with the Judicial system. This "DANCE" includes Motions, Discovery and Plea offers.

During this time you will be given a number of hearings dealing with various motions by you or your attorney. These may occur in the court itself, in which case you will be transported to the Federal Court, in shackles, for the procedure. In some instances these motions or hearings can be conducted by video conferencing from the Detention facility to the Court.

At some point you will decide whether to take a plea offer, if offered by the Prosecutor, or go to trial. This is the most critical decision that you can make throughout the process. If you are truly not guilty your first inclination is to vigorously defend your case in front of a jury.

This could be a devastating mistake and should be carefully considered if a plea deal is offered by the Prosecutor. Juries are often easily persuaded by Prosecutors with even the most seemingly benign evidence or testimony. Remember, if you are found guilty in a jury trial your sentence and fine could easily be twice what the Prosecutor offered in a plea deal!

If you accept a plea you, in essence , have become guilty of the charges brought by the Prosecutor, whatever they may have reduced to. This will set in motion a series of events which will move you to your final destination in the Federal Criminal Justice System, Federal Prison. That is, unless you have been turned to "Informant" or "Snitch" which can mitigate or even eliminate prison time altogether!

Depending on the Crime or Criminal Enterprise and the role that you may have played surrounding this illegal action your testimony may be important enough to bring the Enterprise or one or more of the key figures involved with it to a conviction. Your cooperation with the Government may result in a lower sentence, probation or, if sufficient danger exists to you or your families safety, you could be eligible for the witness protection program.

After the guilty verdict has been rendered a Pre-sentencing Investigation Report will be compiled for the Court. The sentencing judge will review this report along with the Prosecutor's plea offer (which you and he will have signed) and determine the sentence and fine he will impose.

The Probation officer assigned to the case will interview you for this Pre-sentencing Investigation and ask a series of questions related to your education, work history, personal life, criminal record and finances. After this interview they will conduct a background check verifying all of your statements insofar as possible in the time allotted and their workload. Credit checks will be made, schools checked with your grade records, military record, if any and your work history will be confirmed. The IRS will be contacted to confirm that all taxes were paid and current.

Any deviation from your statements to the Probation officer and their findings result in a blemish and the Probation Officer can and will note "Enhancements" to the report. These are points in categories (see the Sentencing Guideline later in this publication) which can add significant more time to your sentence, even after you and the Prosecutor have agreed on these through the plea offer!

- **It is imperative that you obtain a Pre-Sentencing Investigation Report before you accept any Plea Offer! This may affect your decision to accept the Plea offer or go to trial.**

- **If you take a Plea offer and find out later that there were a number of "enhancements" because of the PSI, increasing the expected prison term, you no longer have the option of going to trial!**

After your sentencing hearing you will await disposition by the Bureau of Prisons as to which Federal Facility you will be incarcerated. This could take as long as six months during which time you will still be interred in the Detention Facility.

At some point you will be transferred to Federal Marshals who are responsible for your transport.

The time for the entire process can be as quick as six month to two or three years! Of course, if you opted for a speedy trail or the Prosecutor was expeditious in offering a plea that you found acceptable the time would be shorter.

During this time your finances are going to be seriously tapped and diminished. Your family's needs still go on. Bills still have to paid; rent, car payment, food, utilities, clothing, fuel, education if children are in college, etc.. You will require some money in your account in Detention or prison for essential   and non-essential items not provided.

The Federal Criminal Justice System will financially break the back of nearly all convicted and wreak havoc with family and friends. Of course, the rationale is that "you committed the crime so it is all your fault and the results of your actions"! True, if you are really the "Criminal" the Government says you are.

But if you are caught in the snare of the "War of Drugs" by marijuana being found in a baggie in your vehicle or person, or transmitted information or documents committing wire fraud and are serving upwards of 5 years in prison for these "crimes" or others like them, your life is forever changed by the evil system that is totally out of control!

After you serve your time you will be released to a Probation Officer who is responsible for monitoring your activities. This includes where you live, where you work, where you travel, your regular Urine Analysis tests (UA), bank accounts, etc. You will report to him monthly for at least three years. He will conduct surprise visits to your residence and walk through to verify that no apparent illegal items (firearms, drugs) are laying about. He does not need a warrant to conduct this walkthrough!

Such is the process of anyone indicted or arrested by the Federal Government and most local governments. The flow chart depicted below broadly shows the various steps through the System. Details are offered, sometimes repeated, for emphasis throughout this publication. This is to instill in the reader the pitfalls, sometimes lack of logic and how extensive the Government's zealousness is to bring about a conviction, regardless of the circumstances.

The Sequence of Events in the Criminal Justice System

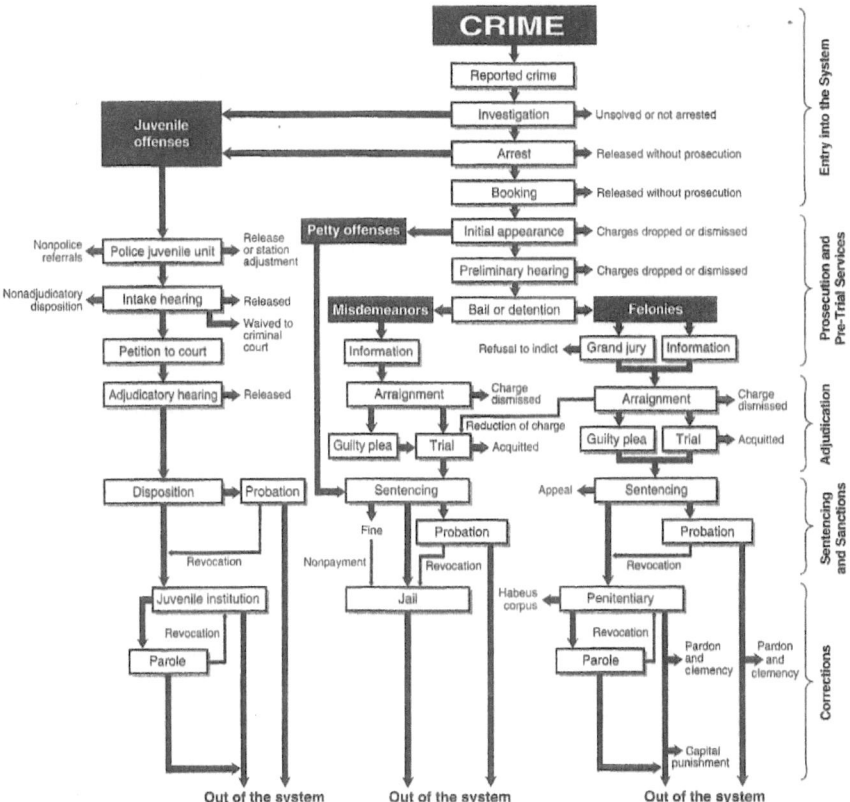

SOURCE: Adapted from *The Challenge of Crime in a Free Society*. President's Commission on Law Enforcement and Administration of Justice, 1967.

Chapter 18

Judges and Judges as Lawyers!

Judges have the power, virtually unlimited power, to set sentences and penalties for any accused brought before them found guilty. Federal judges are appointed by the President for a lifetime position. They are nearly omnipotent in their position and are rarely removed. Most aspire to becoming a Circuit Court Judge or even a Supreme Court Judge.

Federal Judges tend to become tainted with the constant flow of accused felons that come before them. Remember, the Federal Government (Assistant U.S. Attorney's/Prosecutors) have a 97% conviction rate because they "stack" charges and demand a guilty Plea for reduced fines or sentences! Judges, in the back of their mind, sincerely believe that all who come before him accused of a crime are guilty.

Americans do not live under Constitutional Law any longer. The Courts regularly give lip service in many renderings about the Bill of Rights and your Rights under the Constitution. In actuality the Courts treat the Bill of Rights as if they were a privilege to be doled out, a granting or reneging of these "privileges" by the Court or the Prosecutor.

The Criminal Code (Title 18) claims that Federally imposed "guidelines" are required to be used as a standard by Judges in ruling when, in fact, they are merely subterfuge to make you believe that the Judges are constrained to these "guidelines".

Judges consistently use the "guidelines" which are nothing more than another name for the Mandatory Sentencing Requirements overturned by Booker Vs. The United States in the late 2005. The government simply changed the heading, added an upward/downward departure clause and re-published.

SUPREME COURT OF THE UNITED STATES
UNITED STATES *v.* BOOKER
CERTIORARI TO THE UNITED STATES COURT OF APPEALS FOR THE SEVENTH CIRCUIT

No. 04—104.Argued October 4, 2004–Decided January 12, 2005

Under the Federal Sentencing Guidelines, the sentence authorized by the jury verdict in respondent Booker's drug case was 210-to-262 months in prison. At the sentencing hearing, the judge found additional facts by a preponderance of the evidence. Because these findings mandated a sentence between 360 months and life, the judge gave Booker a 30-year sentence instead of the 21-year, 10-month, sentence he could have imposed based on the facts proved to the jury beyond a reasonable doubt.

The Seventh Circuit held that this application of the Guidelines conflicted with the *Apprendi* v. *New Jersey,* 530 U.S. 466, 490, holding that "[other than the fact of a prior conviction, any fact that increases the penalty for a crime beyond the prescribed statutory maximum must be submitted to a jury, and proved beyond a reasonable doubt." Relying on *Blakely* v. *Washington,* 542 U.S. ___, the court held that the sentence violated the Sixth Amendment and instructed the District Court either to sentence Booker within the sentencing range supported by the jury's findings or to hold a separate sentencing hearing before a jury. In respondent Fanfan's case, the maximum sentence authorized by the jury verdict under the Guidelines was 78 months in prison. At the sentencing hearing, the District Judge found by a preponderance of the evidence additional facts authorizing a sentence in the 188-to-235-month range, which would have required him to impose a 15- or 16-year sentence instead of the 5 or 6 years authorized by the jury verdict alone.

Relying on *Blakely*'s majority opinion, statements in its dissenting opinions, and the Solicitor General's brief in *Blakely,* the judge concluded that he could not follow the Guidelines and imposed a sentence based solely upon the guilty verdict in the case. The Government filed a notice of appeal in the First Circuit and a petition for certiorari before judgment in this Court. *Held:* **The judgment of the Court of Appeals in No. 04—104 is affirmed, and the case is remanded. The judgment of the District Court in No. 04—105 is vacated, and the case is remanded.**

Back to review the High Priest:

As rare as this remand was, the bottom line is that the Judge is the HIGH PRIEST of the Government, appointed for life by the Government to impose it's will upon all who are brought before him.

He sits at the "Bench" , an elevated platform with a gavel and flags behind him assuring you that he represents the Government in every rendering.

He wears a black robe like a HIGH PRIEST and the court room has the decorum of a sanctified church.......quiet, lots of oak or mahogany paneling and a near subservient demeanor, all but bowing before this HIGH PRIEST!

No one dare to disrespect this HIGH PRIEST or he will reprimand any and all who do, with certain deference to the Prosecutor! After all , these two are in collusion and like-mindedness as far as all accused brought before them. The judge will fine any and all who he perceives has "contempt" for the Court (himself) and will even send them to jail indefinitely if he perceives that the "contempt" was egregious enough!

While the Judge is to be the arbiter between the Prosecuting and Defending Parties he often acts as attorney from the bench. How does he do this? By offering advice and suggesting tactics, remedies or other charges that might be brought by the Prosecutor in the Courtroom venue! He, by law and ethics, is prohibited from doing this but Federal Judges regularly do this thus practice law from the bench. And no one, but no one challenges this!

Why? The Judge nearly always makes his comments to the Prosecutor who is glad to have more ammunition with which to bring about a conviction and longer sentence. The Defense attorney is afraid to affect his standing with the Court.

Never forget, the Lawyer/Attorneys' first obligation is to the United States Government. His second obligation is to the Court. His last and final obligation is to you, his employer, whom he is defending for your freedom. You are his last consideration and he will never jeopardize his standing in the court over you or anyone else. He, too, must lick the boot of the HIGH PRIEST JUDGE who can and will impose the harshest sentence he can get away with.

No sitting Judge wants his rulings overturned on Appeal. Even though the Judge profession is the good old boys club and they usually look out for one another, they do want to follow a semblance of the letter of the law when proceedings are being conducted and when your "due process" is being carried out and when they impose sentences.

The following article offers some hope to felons convicted in the future. The Court almost never revisits prior cases in an attempt to rectify past misdeeds!

A4 | Monday, June 29, 2009

Judge: Sentencing can better fit crime's circumstances

The Associated Press

ABERDEEN — A federal judge in South Dakota says he and his colleagues are now more able to craft what they determine to be more appropriate sentences after nearly 20 years of having limited freedom to punish criminals as they see fit.

Judges must look at a variety of factors to determine a sentencing range after somebody is found guilty or admits to a crime. But thanks to two U.S. Supreme Court decisions in recent years, they now have had increased power to sentence criminals to more or less time in prison, depending on a crime's circumstances.

Aberdeen-based Judge Charles B. Kornmann said that's good, as under the old mandate, he sometimes had to hand out sentences that were obviously too severe.

During a 2003 sentencing hearing, a defendant faced the prospect of life in prison in a drug distribution case. At the time, Kornmann called the guidelines "outrageous" and sentenced the defendant to 20 years.

U.S. Sentencing Commission Guidelines took effect in 1987, and the only instances in which they could be set aside involved considerable extenuating circumstances.

Some federal judges, including Kornmann, started varying from the mandated sentence ranges as early as 2004, when the Washington Supreme Court ruled them unconstitutional.

A 2007 U.S. Supreme Court ruling ended the practice of some judges using the sentencing ranges as mandates, while others issued their own sentences.

Kornmann said most sentences probably still fall within the guidelines, but there are cases in which they just don't make sense. Ranges are based upon an individual's criminal history, cooperation with law enforcement and any admission of guilt. The data is gathered in a presentence report and forwarded to the judge.

Judges can also consider such other factors as:

¶ The need to reflect the seriousness of the offense, to promote respect for the law and to provide just punishment.

¶ The ability to afford adequate deterrence to criminal conduct.

¶ Protecting the public from further crimes by the defendant.

¶ Providing the defendant with needed education or vocational training, medical care or other correctional treatment.

¶ The need to avoid unwarranted sentence disparities among defendants with similar records who have been found guilty of similar conduct.

¶ The need to provide restitution to victims.

You see, Prosecutors aren't satisfied that they were able to get a conviction. They want the longest sentence possible imposed unless they plead the defendant on some sort of "deal". So, if the Judge doesn't follow the "guidelines" by giving a lower sentence, the Prosecutor, yes the Prosecutor, can and will Appeal to the higher court for a more severe sentence!

Of course, if the Judge gives a higher sentence the Prosecutor is delighted. Your appeal for the lower sentence will go on deaf ears even if heard later by the Appellate Court!

Your case stays with the Court even after your incarceration and during **Probation, which is always imposed by the Judge.**

It is not enough that you "pay your debt to society" by the sentence rendered and time served. You are compelled to generally serve another three years of Probation under jurisdiction of the Court/Judge that sentenced you. While on Probation you will be under the direct Supervision of a Federal Probation Officer who reports to the Court.

Chapter 19
Motions and Briefs

As time passes you or your attorney will submit a series of Motions to the court. A **legal motion** is a procedural device in law to bring a limited, contested issue before a court for decision. A motion may be thought of as a request to the judge (or judges) to make a decision about the case.

Pre-trial motions are made by the prosecution and the defense before the trial begins, and can deal with a variety of issues. Common types of pre-trial motions include motions to exclude certain evidence from trial, motions to prevent certain witnesses from testifying, and motions that the case should be dismissed for some legal reason.

Motions may be made in the form of an oral request in open court, which is then summarily granted or denied orally. But today, most motions (especially on dispositive issues that could decide the entire case) are decided after oral argument preceded by the filing and service of legal papers.

At some point the **Statute of Limitations** for any crime that you are accused of that occurred long in the past may become an issue, except for murder. Seven years is usually the median time where a charge cannot be brought against you for a crime committed in the past. The Statute of Limitations for some crimes are as low as three years in the past up to ten years.

A "**motion to dismiss**" could be filed because the Prosecutor filed charges after the Statute of Limitations has past on the charge. The court can Dismiss without any evidence having been presented by the Prosecution.

Motion for Change of Venue
A motion for Change of Venue would be made to move the Defendant to another location far from the current jurisdiction. This would be filed in the case of a notorious crime, local celebrity or where media attention is so profound that a fair and unbiased jury could not be selected.

Motion to Quash
This motion would be made by the Defense to prevent witnesses, certain evidence and documents from being used by the Prosecution , either contained in the filing of deciding whether the defendant is guilty or not guilty of committing that crime. It is at this time your attorney should pay close attention to the judges instructions. It is possible for the Judges instructions to be so restrictive that the jurors have no choice but to convict.
 legal documents with the court or at trial.

Motion in limine
A "**motion *in limine***" asks the court to decide that certain evidence may or may not be presented to the jury at the trial. A motion in limine generally addresses issues which would be prejudicial for the jury to hear in open court, even if the other side makes a timely objection which is sustained, and the judge instructs the jury to disregard the evidence.

For example, the defendant may ask the court to rule that evidence of a prior conviction that occurred a long time ago should not be allowed into evidence at the trial because it would be more prejudicial than probative. If the motion is granted, then evidence regarding the conviction could not be mentioned in front of the jury, without first approaching the judge outside of the hearing of the jury and obtaining permission. The violation of a motion in limine can result in the court declaring a mistrial.

There are three types of Motions in Limine:

1. Inclusionary - A motion asking the court to have something included in the trial.
2. Exclusionary - A motion asking the court to have something excluded in the trial.
3. Preclusionary - A motion asking the court to have something precluded in the trial

Motion for a directed verdict
A "**motion for a directed verdict**" asks the court to rule that the prosecutor has not proven their case, and there is no need for the defense to attempt to present evidence, prior to the defense presenting any evidence. If granted, the court would dismiss the case.

Motion for judgment n.o.v.
A "**motion for judgment *n.o.v.*" (*non obstante veredicto*, or notwithstanding the verdict) asks the court to reverse the jury's verdict on the grounds that the jury could not reasonably have reached such a verdict. This motion is made after the jury's verdict. If granted, the court enters a new verdict. Typically, this motion can be used in a criminal case *only to reverse a guilty verdict; not guilty verdicts are immune to reversal by the court.*

Motion for nolle prosequi
A "**motion for *nolle prosequi*"** ("not prosecuting") is a motion by a prosecutor or defendant to drop legal charges, usually in exchange for cooperation or informing.

Motion to compel
A "**motion to compel**" asks the court to order either the opposing party or a third party to take some action. This sort of motion most commonly deals with discovery disputes, when a party who has propounded discovery to either the opposing party or a third party believes that the discovery responses are insufficient. The motion to compel is used to ask the court to order the non-complying party to produce the documentation or information requested, and/or to sanction the non-complying party for their failure to comply with the discovery requests.

Motion for new trial
A **motion for new trial** asks to overturn or set aside a court's decision or jury verdict. Such a motion is proposed by a party who is dissatisfied with the end result of a case. This motion must be based on some vital error in the court's handling of the trial, such as the admission or exclusion of key evidence, or an incorrect instruction to the jury.

Generally the motion is filed within a short time after the trial (7–30 days) and is decided prior to the lodging of an appeal. In some jurisdictions, a motion for new trial which is not ruled upon by a set period of time automatically is deemed to be denied.

Briefs are filed with the Court citing case law(s) related to the defendants case in an attempt to obtain a favorable ruling. These are usually filed to challenge charges, allegations, evidence and other finer points of law used against the defendant.

Rebuttals are submitted to the Court from the Prosecutor on Motions and Briefs filed by the Defendant. Based upon the Judges understanding of the law and his interpretation as to the relevancy of these citations to the case at hand he will rule. His ruling is final and can only be set aside during the Appeal Process if the Defendant is convicted and if he wins his Appeal.

If a Plea offer has been refused by the accused or if none were offered by the Prosecutor you will go to trial.

Chapter 20

Deal or No Deal! Risks!

"Feds Often Give Leniency For Guilty Pleas, Especially When Paid For!"

Federal prosecutors often cut deals with serious criminals, including murderers, drug dealers and gang members, offering leniency in exchange for a guilty plea and testimony in court, *The Baltimore Sun* reported (baltimoresun.com).in the first quarter of this year, 96% of federal cases garnered guilty Pleas, the newspaper said, citing data from the U.S. Sentencing Commission. Defense attorneys say it gives Cooperators (read snitch) incentive to lie. "Their testimony is essentially bought and paid for ", John Wesley Hall, president of the National Association of Criminal Defense Lawyers, told the *Sun.*

Prosecutors tell the *Sun* that the deals are necessary to get information about criminal groups. " Often the people who are in the best position to be witnesses in a case are the people who, themselves, have been involved in criminal activity", Maryland U.S. Attorney Rod Rothstein said.

Regardless, the Judge may or not accept any plea offer made by the Prosecutor and agreed upon by the accused. Unless the Judge signs a legal document sometimes called an 11(c) prior to any agreement between the parties he is under no obligation to honor the agreement!

By accepting any Plea offer you will plead guilty and will not go to a jury trial. Your case will be disposed of forthwith. The Pre-sentence Investigation will commence and your Sentencing Hearing will be scheduled.

If your "Deal" consists on informing on others whom you had conspired with or have knowledge of their criminal activity and the Judge still sentences you to serve time in a Federal Facility the knowledge of this "cooperation" with the Feds will follow you into Prison. It will not take long for your fellow convicts to find out that you have been a snitch or informant. This does not bode well for anyone incarcerated. No one, but no one cottons to informants and great bodily harm comes to those who are.

Chapter 21

Trial by Jury: Risky Business!

Rejecting any Plea offer and **going to trial** is always an option but carries with it some risk, sometimes substantial risk.

In a criminal trial the judge or a jury decides whether the defendant committed the crime. The standard used in criminal cases is "beyond a reasonable doubt" - that is, there is no reasonable doubt in the judge or jurors' minds that the defendant committed the crime.

A **speedy trial** may or may not be to your benefit. If, for example, the Prosecutor obtained an Indictment against you with little or no solid evidence, it may be in your best interest to go to trial as quickly as possible. You or your lawyer can determine from the Discovery Process whether the Prosecution has sufficient evidence to win a conviction if your charges were brought before a jury.

Discovery will also determine whether or not you want to waive your right to a speedy trial in the hopes that, over time, witnesses may move or disappear, evidence is lost or tainted in some way and that flaws can be found in certain potential testimony.

You may want to accept a Plea offer from the Prosecution or, even that your attorney suggest one to the Prosecutor. To plead guilty without a plea offer is foolhardy unless there is no other option available.

A criminal trial has several phases:

- Jury selection - A pool of potential jurors is gathered, and asked a number of questions. The prosecution and defense each can choose to exclude a certain number of people from the jury. **This process is called voir dire.** Questions to potential jurors are submitted in writing to the Judge, by the Prosecutor and the Defense attorney prior to questioning of the jury. The Judge must approve all questions to jurors by the parties.

  Potential jurors with criminal backgrounds, relatives in Law Enforcement or Government, biases or prejudices are generally excused from serving. Questions designed by both sides are, naturally, structured to select the most likely candidates on the jury to favor their case. While not an exact science, questions can be framed in such a way to give some indication as how the juror may behave in his thinking as evidence and "facts" are presented.

- Opening statements - Each side presents an overview of the case, from their perspective. The prosecution goes first, followed by the defense. Each side will make claims that should be proven as the trial proceeds.

- Witness testimony - Each side can call witnesses and ask them questions about the case and/or the defendant. First, the prosecution calls their witnesses, who can then be cross examined by the defense. Then, the defense calls their witnesses, who can be cross examined by the prosecution. The Prosecution often uses informants or 'Snitches" to testify against the accused. This has been cover in other chapters.

- Closing arguments - The prosecution, and then the defense, make a brief statement summarizing their side of the case. All defects in the Prosecutions case should be emphasized at this time to place the notion of **Reasonable Doubt** in any one of the jurors thinking.

  One juror can deadlock a verdict, result in a mistrial or "hung jury". At trial, unless there is clear and compelling evidence that you, the accused, are innocent your only hope of an acquittal or dismissal is REASONABLE DOUBT. This is the strategy your attorney must take when there is any doubt of the outcome of your trial.

- Jury Instruction - The judge addresses the jurors, explaining to them the crime the defendant was charged with, and the legal standard they must apply when deciding whether the defendant is guilty or not guilty of committing that crime. It is at this time your attorney should pay close attention to the judges instructions. It is possible for the Judges instructions to be so restrictive that the jurors have no choice but to convict.

- **Jury nullification-** A jury can acquit a defendant despite the weight of evidence against him or her. It is any rendering of a verdict by a trial jury which acquits a criminal defendant despite that defendant's violation of the letter of the law—that is, of an official rule, and especially a legislative enactment. The jury may find that the law is too vague, too severe for the offense or some other mitigating factor to render this decision.

In the rare instances where this occurs the Judge will generally overrule the verdict or may declare a mistrial.

After months, sometimes years, of Detention or free on bond the trial phase usually lasts a few days or a couple of weeks. Highly visible personalities or notorious crimes can result in trials lasting several weeks. The O.J. Simpson trial is one case in point.

Chapter 22

The Verdict. Now What?

The jury weighs the evidence presented, applies the proper legal standard, and decides whether the defendant is guilty or not guilty. In a criminal trial all jurors must agree on the verdict whether guilty or innocent.

If the jury renders a verdict of NOT GUILTY you will be released immediately from custody and from bail. Of course, you will receive no compensation, apology or any other such platitude from the Court or the Prosecutor for the terrible inconvenience or financial losses that you suffered.

This does not mean that you are free and clear from future charges that the Prosecutor may levy against you. He may gather or find new evidence, pay or locate an informant or file slightly different charges so as not to place you in DOUBLE JEOPARDY. It depends on how much the Prosecutor wants a conviction and, especially, how badly he wants to convict YOU!

Human nature, being what it is, will still leave lingering doubts from some family members, co-workers and friends about any role you MIGHT have played in whatever crime you were charged with. No amount of explanation or rationale will stem this. Unless you have had the full support of these individuals throughout your ordeal it will take time to reduce or eliminate these doubts.

If you are found guilty and have been free on bond the judge may or may not revoke the bond to have you in custody awaiting sentencing. You will be required to an interview with the Probation Officer for the Pre-sentencing Investigation. You must attend any and all hearings that the Court may require. Sometimes your attorney may attend for you. Any remission on your part could result in a bench warrant issued by the Court and further charges brought against you or your bond revoked.

If you have been in custody, after the verdict you will be immediately returned to Detention until the PSI is conducted and the sentencing hearing scheduled. This entire process usually takes two month to six months, depending on the severity of the crime. Wait, wait and more wait!

Chapter 23

The Pre-Sentence Investigation

While it may seem to be anti-climatic to the entire ordeal that has just been concluded, the PSI is a very important phase of the Process. It is during this time that you will be gauged on the truthfulness of the information that you provide during the interview by the Probation Officer assigned to your case by the Court.

Your prior criminal record plays a very crucial role in how the judge will sentence you to the Guidelines. The crime that you were convicted of carries with it a certain number of "points" . These points will place you at a sentencing level (see Chart in next chapter). That may not be the only time that you will serve!

Based upon your prior activities you will be "enhanced" with additional prison time. If there are no outstanding blemishes on your record or even in your life, you will not be "enhanced". If there are, you could receive additional time amounting to several years.

Those designated "Career Criminal" who have a sordid and extensive past committing various crimes are especially enhanced and can have 10 or more years added to their sentence. As few as four or five instances of "crime" can place someone in the Career Criminal category.

That is why it is imperative to press for the Pre-sentencing Investigation before you accept any plea offer from a Prosecutor. You may have nothing to lose by going to trial and hope for a hung jury or reasonable doubt acquittal verdict.

Moreover, you can derive some consolation and pleasure that you are tying up the System and its resources for some period of time while the Prosecutor and his team prepare their case and the Court itself is losing many other opportunities to process other individuals though motions and hearings! Of course, *if you are paying a lawyer* you are going to incur unbelievable costs going to trial!

Chapter 24

Sentencing and the "Guidelines"
Beware of the "Enhancements"!

If a person is convicted of a crime, either by a plea bargain or by a trial, the term "sentencing" refers to how they are punished. In some cases, sentencing occurs after the plea bargain or verdict. In more complicated cases, a separate hearing is held on the issue of sentencing, and the judge hears arguments from both sides as to what the proper punishment should be.

For some crimes, sentencing is explicitly stated by the law, and the judge has limited discretion *(Not necessarily so. He has full discretion!)* For other crimes, the judge has wide discretion in determining the proper punishment. Types of punishments can include fines, prison time, and restitution (paying back money that was stolen, or compensating the victim for property that was damaged or destroyed).

Fines and restitution are often so high that they can never be paid by the "criminal". The Government has billions of dollars owed by convicted felons that they use as collateral for securities that they issue through the Federal Reserve Bank and the Department of Treasury.

The law says that Judges cannot take into consideration character references, favorable career, life or good things that defendant has accomplished, military record or any other favorable factor when sentencing! Even though your attorney may want to bring in character references, letters of recommendation and military record into any hearing or pleas to the judge for leniency it will fall on deaf ears. The judge is only interest in the here and now, the crime and you as the perpetrator!

The entire time that you were detained in a facility awaiting disposition of your case may or may not be applied to the time of sentence you must serve. Sometimes the Court and the BOP takes the position that your time starts the moment of your sentence, not when you were arrested and placed in Detention.

Remember, you could spend as long a two years in Detention awaiting disposition of your case. It seems as though the Court and the BOP have equal authority to determine the time that you must serve and what the "start" time is.

If you have accepted a Plea offer from the Prosecutor, it usually comes with a "point" reduction of three (3) "points" for taking responsibility for your crime. When you are sentenced at your hearing you will allocute your guilt to the judge thus sealing your point reduction. Often, the point reduction is offset by the enhancements applied through the criminal history category, a zero sum game.

Criminal History can include such minor traffic violations such as speeding, eluding and driving while suspended. Others, such as domestic violence, soliciting, writing a check on insufficient funds and failure to file an income tax return can result in points added to the Criminal History moving you up a category or two thus adding time to your sentence.

Please note that Zones A, B or C Offence Levels shown below are rarely, if ever, found in sentencing a convicted felon. They may be achieved by point reduction due to plea or taking responsibility.

Downward and **Upward Departure** awards are simply applying either the minimum or maximum time under the offense level to the sentence. These are sometimes negotiable with the Prosecutor or Judge. Negotiate all that you can to get what you can!

If you had several charges brought against you and you were found guilty on more than one of them the Federal Government may elect to sentence you *consecutively* for each charge. This could result in a significant number of years in prison. You will serve the sentence on one charge before the term begins on the other charge(s)!

If, however, the Feds sentence you to *concurrent* sentences for multiple charges you will serve the longest of them while the others are served within that term. How that determination is made is somewhat of a mystery from case to case.

If you are sentenced and /or serving in a state case while your Federal case is pending the Feds will usually take jurisdiction and remove you from the state system where you will then serve Federal time while the state sentence becomes concurrent with your Fed time.

Either the state or the Federal Government can file new charges against you at any time while you are incarcerated. These may be prosecuted while you are serving time or when you are released.

SENTENCING TABLE
(in months of imprisonment)

		Criminal History Category (Criminal History Points)					
	Offense Level	I (0 or 1)	II (2 or 3)	III (4, 5, 6)	IV (7, 8, 9)	V (10, 11, 12)	VI (13 or more)
	1	0-6	0-6	0-6	0-6	0-6	0-6
	2	0-6	0-6	0-6	0-6	0-6	1-7
	3	0-6	0-6	0-6	0-6	2-8	3-9
	4	0-6	0-6	0-6	2-8	4-10	6-12
Zone A	5	0-6	0-6	1-7	4-10	6-12	9-15
	6	0-6	1-7	2-8	6-12	9-15	12-18
	7	0-6	2-8	4-10	8-14	12-18	15-21
	8	0-6	4-10	6-12	10-16	15-21	18-24
Zone B	9	4-10	6-12	8-14	12-18	18-24	21-27
	10	6-12	8-14	10-16	15-21	21-27	24-30
Zone C	11	8-14	10-16	12-18	18-24	24-30	27-33
	12	10-16	12-18	15-21	21-27	27-33	30-37
	13	12-18	15-21	18-24	24-30	30-37	33-41
	14	15-21	18-24	21-27	27-33	33-41	37-46
	15	18-24	21-27	24-30	30-37	37-46	41-51
	16	21-27	24-30	27-33	33-41	41-51	46-57
	17	24-30	27-33	30-37	37-46	46-57	51-63
	18	27-33	30-37	33-41	41-51	51-63	57-71
	19	30-37	33-41	37-46	46-57	57-71	63-78
	20	33-41	37-46	41-51	51-63	63-78	70-87
Zone D	21	37-46	41-51	46-57	57-71	70-87	77-96
	22	41-51	46-57	51-63	63-78	77-96	84-105
	23	46-57	51-63	57-71	70-87	84-105	92-115
	24	51-63	57-71	63-78	77-96	92-115	100-125
	25	57-71	63-78	70-87	84-105	100-125	110-137
	26	63-78	70-87	78-97	92-115	110-137	120-150
	27	70-87	78-97	87-108	100-125	120-150	130-162
	28	78-97	87-108	97-121	110-137	130-162	140-175
	29	87-108	97-121	108-135	121-151	140-175	151-188
	30	97-121	108-135	121-151	135-168	151-188	168-210
	31	108-135	121-151	135-168	151-188	168-210	188-235
	32	121-151	135-168	151-188	168-210	188-235	210-262
	33	135-168	151-188	168-210	188-235	210-262	235-293
	34	151-188	168-210	188-235	210-262	235-293	262-327
	35	168-210	188-235	210-262	235-293	262-327	292-365
	36	188-235	210-262	235-293	262-327	292-365	324-405
	37	210-262	235-293	262-327	292-365	324-405	360-life
	38	235-293	262-327	292-365	324-405	360-life	360-life
	39	262-327	292-365	324-405	360-life	360-life	360-life
	40	292-365	324-405	360-life	360-life	360-life	360-life
	41	324-405	360-life	360-life	360-life	360-life	360-life
	42	360-life	360-life	360-life	360-life	360-life	360-life
	43	life	life	life	life	life	life

Good Time Out Date

After sentencing, the Department of Justice will determine a Good Time Out Date for each convicted felon. There is no longer parole in the Federal system. All inmates must serve 85% of their sentence unless overturned on appeal. The good time out date is determined from when the

Court ruled that your sentence actually began. For example, you may have been arrested and detained for a number of months before the disposition of your case. The Judge or the BOP may rule that all or part of that time will apply to your sentence. If you have been free on bail/bond awaiting disposition of your case none of that time will be allocated to your sentence.

If you had been held or convicted in another jurisdiction or had state charges pending you may or may not have any detention or jail time allocated to your Federal sentence. The Federal Government trumps the States so you may be able to serve State and Federal prison sentences concurrently in the Federal system if the Feds take you from the State.

If you have state charges pending you must serve your Federal sentence before the state can take you for their sentencing term of prison.

You can only lose time on your good time out date. You will not get any more. It is not difficult to lose good time. Infractions can take as many as several months from that time.

Prisoners having very long sentences naturally have more good time potential in the number of days or months that is applied. Good time out date becomes more important to convicted felons as that date begins to arrive.

Inmates serving time in a high security facility due to the severity of their crimes often lose all of their good time because of fighting, assault or disobeying rules.

Chapter 25

Where to now?

The Federal Bureau of Prisons (BOP) operates 114 Facilities across the country. Some "compounds" are multiple housing units with various levels of security. Depending on the "points" a convicted felon has amassed due to his crime or crimes, he will assigned to a facility with a specified security level. Felons with a history of violence will generally have the highest points and be incarcerated in the highest security facilities.

There are far more State prisons than Federal and the conditions generally run worse than any Federal facility. Moreover, many facilities are run by Corporations such as CCA (Corrections Corporation of America). You do not want to be detained in CCA facility! The staff, food and medical care are usually sub-par even though they have to meet minimum Federal standards.

As the inmate serves his time it is possible for him to reduce his "points" based upon a number of factors. Conduct, programming in various classes, work ethic and other factors can reduce his points. As points get lower over time he will transfer to lower and lower security facilities

Felons convicted of heinous crimes such as acts of terrorism, serial killers, bombers and other notorious acts of violence are sentences to life in Administrative Facilities such as the SuperMax (ADX) at Florence, Colorado and others. These convicts will never have their points lowered and will never transfer to a lower security facility.

The BOP categorizes their various security facilities in the following manner.

Minimum Security
Minimum security institutions, also known as Federal Prison Camps (**FPCs**), have dormitory housing, a relatively low staff-to-inmate ratio, and limited or no perimeter fencing. These institutions are work- and program-oriented; and many are located adjacent to larger institutions or on military bases, where inmates help serve the labor needs of the larger institution or base.

Low Security
Low security Federal Correctional Institutions (**FCIs**) have double-fenced perimeters, mostly dormitory or cubicle housing, and strong work and program components. The staff-to-inmate ratio in these institutions is higher than in minimum security facilities.

Medium Security

Medium security FCI's (and USPs designated to house medium security inmates) have strengthened perimeters, often double fences with electronic detection systems), mostly cell-type housing, a wide variety of work and treatment programs, an even higher staff to inmate ratio than low security FCIs, and even greater internal controls.

High Security

High security institutions, also known as United States Penitentiaries (**USPs**), have highly-secured perimeters (featuring walls or reinforced fences), multiple- and single-occupant cell housing, the highest staff-to-inmate ratio, and close control of inmate movement.

Correctional Complexes

A number of BOP institutions belong to Federal Correctional Complexes (**FCCs**). At FCCs, institutions with different missions and security levels are located in close proximity to one another. FCCs increase efficiency through the sharing of services, enable staff to gain experience at institutions of many security levels, and enhance emergency preparedness by having additional resources within close proximity.

Administrative

Administrative facilities are institutions with special missions, such as the detention of pretrial offenders; the treatment of inmates with serious or chronic medical problems; or the containment of extremely dangerous, violent, or escape-prone inmates. Administrative facilities include Metropolitan Correctional Centers (**MCCs**), Metropolitan Detention Centers (**MDCs**), Federal Detention Centers (**FDCs**), and Federal Medical Centers (**FMCs**), as well as the Federal Transfer Center (**FTC**), the Medical Center for Federal Prisoners (**MCFP**), and the Administrative-Maximum (**ADX**) U.S. Penitentiary. Administrative facilities are capable of holding inmates in all security categories.

A convicted felon will **usually** serve time at a facility within 500 miles of home or his family. However, the BOP regularly moves prisoners from facility to facility and, often, across the country from home! There appears to be no rhyme or reason for many of these transfers.

After sentencing the "convict" may spend several weeks in detention awaiting transportation to his assigned BOP facility. These assignments are made by the Bureau of Prison (BOP) after the judge in the case has forwarded the details of the case and the sentence to the Department of Justice.

As the felon is moved from the jurisdiction where he was convicted and detained he will be transported first by the correctional facility where he has been detained. Every movement is carefully supervised and the prisoner is shackled hands and feet. No advance notice is given to the prisoner when he will be moved, ever. He is usually awakened in the early morning, taken to a holding cell where he is fed, clothing changed, shackled and placed in a vehicle for transport.

At some point the will be transferred to the United States Marshals Service where they will return shackles to the delivering authority and re-shackle the prisoner with their hardware.

The prisoner is now transported by Federal Marshals by ground or air, depending on where he is going. Most will travel by "Con Air", one of three Boeing 737's operated by the Marshals Service, and sometimes in a smaller aircraft operated from time to time under special circumstances. These all route through the BOP routing facility in Oklahoma City, near the center of the country.

The aircraft makes several stops throughout any given weekday, picking up prisoners from various regions and cities, occasionally dropping others off to go to their assigned prisons.

Other prisoners will travel by van, bus or train to their ultimate BOP facility with a U.S. Marshall escort, especially if they are closer than 500 miles from their detention facility. If an overnight stop is required the prisoner will be taken to a city or county jail located along the way and he will spend the night there in a cell.

The U.S. Marshals Service aircraft usually arrives at the Oklahoma City facility late afternoon, early evening after several stops around the country. The 200 or so transported prisoners are taken directly off the aircraft into the "concourse" of the BOP facility located across the runway from the regular airport commercial facilities. The prisoner is herded with the others through Receiving where he is unshackled, strip searched including orifices, given a change of clothing and interviewed. Any medical needs will be addressed at that time.

The prisoners are then assigned a floor, Pod and cell. The Pod houses some 80 to 120 inmates in two man cells. The cells have bunk beds and a small table, toilet and sink. An already housed prisoner usually gets the bottom bunk unless the new prisoner has medical problems where he is unable to climb into the top bunk. Showers are located on the corners of each floor.

Each inmate is assigned chores such as sweeping, mopping, serving food and clean up after meals. There are at least three television rooms around each Pod, each TV usually turned to different programming; sports, news, Spanish speaking, sit-coms or movies. Who watches what can sometimes be a bone a contention among the inmates. The correctional officers (CO's) keep the remote and the televisions cannot be changed by the inmate. They must ask permission for channel changes.

Book carts have reading material for the inmate. Religious services are offered on Sunday. There is no outdoor recreation or "yard" at the Oklahoma facility. Inmates so inclined usually walk around the Pod for exercise or do pushups in their cells.

All inmates are locked in their cells at night and allowed into the Pod each morning and throughout the day for meals, work and relaxation. Meals are brought to the Pod morning, afternoon and evening. These are handed out to each inmate. Tables are available in the Pod for eating and relaxing afterward. Medical will bring prescriptions and medications morning and evening to those inmates requiring them.

Inmates are housed in Oklahoma City as little as 5 days to as much as 8 weeks awaiting transportation to their assigned facility. There seems to be no rhyme or reason for the delay.

Prisoners who have been convicted of lesser crimes, have been out on bond during their trial or other disposition are often allowed to self surrender at a specified BOP facility. Others, who have been already incarcerated in a minimum security BOP facility are sometimes permitted to self transport from one facility to another if they have been re-assigned.

Chapter 26

What to expect inside

Correctional Facilities have nothing to do with "correction". Punishment is the byword. Rehabilitation is a farce. The public wants and expects its sociopaths convicted of crime to spend time in prison with the least amount of privilege and as little comfort as possible.

As the Government built more and more prisons over the years they modernized the facilities with better recreation, day rooms and other amenities not available in the older facilities.

It gives some the impression that convicts/inmates live and eat better than many of our unfortunates in society. In some ways this is true. Three nourishing meals are served each and every day. Showers and clean clothes are always available. TV is available and, in state facilities and in SuperMax Federal facilities, an inmate can have his very own TV if he is able to afford one.

The inmate is usually required to work for which he will receive a stipend of some $.10 per hour up to $1.00 or so per hour for wages.

Recreation in the form of weight rooms, library, chapel, basketball, soccer, softball, track, arts and crafts and board games are prevalent in all facilities. All may partake of these activities excepting those confines in Special Housing Units (SHU), called either solitary, segregation or the HOLE! All activity there is limited to a book or two a week and one hour per day to walk in a caged area.

So, yes, inmates do have a better lot in life than many poor people on the outside, thanks to the efforts of liberal lawyers and bleeding heart congressmen. Compared to the stark images given to us in the movies about Sing Sing, Alcatraz and San Quentin the facilities of today are pristine, comfortable and clean.

The loss of freedom, lack of female contact, restrictions on movements and the large number of rules and regulations separates the prisoner from society. Worse, in the higher security facilities where the more violent are housed there is always the risk of   assault and racial outbreaks.

When you arrive at your assigned prison or camp you will be processed into the facility and begin to serve your sentence. After your sentence you are now the property of the Federal Bureau of Prisons (BOP). They have assigned you to particular facility based upon factors that may or may not ever become apparent to you.

The BOP makes its determination on the type of facility where you will serve your time by the number of "points" you have on your record. The higher the point level the more secure the facility with greater restrictions on the prisoner.

You will not be able to change facilities to get closer to your home for at least 18 months and, only then, if you have been assigned to a Camp or low security prison.

R & D:

Receiving and Departure. You will be stripped and cavity searched, photographed, fingerprinted, identification card issued and given a change of clothing to the standard prison garb of the facility. Every tattoo will be photographed to ascertain if any represent a gang or ideological affiliation.

You will be issued shirts, pants, belt, under shirts, under pants, socks and shoes. In addition, you will receive sheets, blanket and pillow for your bunk. You will be provided food and drink, depending upon the time of arrival. This is usually a sandwich, a piece of fruit and water. A package with a bare amount of toiletries will be issued to you.

The only personal belongings that you are permitted to keep are a wedding ring, eye glasses and a small, inexpensive religious medallion. All other items such as watches, radios, tennis shoes, sweats, etc. must be surrendered to either be sent home or donated. The BOP will not store these items for you. Any money that you may have or was in your account at another facility must be forwarded to your "Commissary Account". Under no circumstance is any money permitted in prison.

A cursory medical exam will be scheduled for you shortly after your arrival and you will be questioned about current or recent past injuries or afflictions that you may have. If you have been in detention or another facility a medical exam will have been performed on a regular basis and your records will follow you wherever you go. Any medications that you are authorized to take will be made available to you through the morning and evening sick call or pill line.

If your illnesses are critical enough you may be sent to a facility that provides specialized medical treatment such as Rochester, Minnesota or Buckner North Carolina.

Building, Cell and Bunk Assignment:

A prison counselor will be assigned to you who will review your case and criminal history and make a determination where you will be housed. If you are in any other type of facility but a Camp you will be housed in a POD or a cell among other cells on various levels in the unit.

Your specific bunk assignment will be made by the Counselor or the Correction Officer on duty. Your cell will have a bunk bed, a combination stainless steel toilet and sink, a locker or property box and a small table. You have no choice about whom you will bunk with unless there is a serious conflict that may develop after your arrival.

If you are assigned to a Camp you will usually be housed in a "dormitory" with two man low walled cubicles. As of this date the point level to qualify for a Camp is ten. It was as low as six but very few non-violent, good behavior prisoners were qualifying for a Camp and continued to be housed in higher security facilities.

Counselor, Team Leader, Unit Manager:

Shortly after your arrival, usually within a week, you will receive an orientation by your counselor. Sometimes these are scheduled with other prison staff. At this orientation you will be informed of critical rules and regulations that must be followed, the time of meals, movements allowed, services available and a myriad of other topics.

You will meet with your counselor on a regular basis to discuss your work, activities, programming, point status and family issues. He will update your file with this information for future reference. Your file follows you to each and every facility from the time you were initially arrested.

Any contact between you and your counselor after orientation is made with you sending a "cop out" or "kite" to him with your request. He can take up to 30 days to respond. His response may be to extend his response another 30 days if it is an issue that appears to be frivolous or non-essential. Ultimately you will receive and answer and it is usually negative.

If you are not satisfied with his response you can then move up the chain of command by sending a BP 8. This is reviewed by prison authorities who usually extend it 30 days or more before responding. It is usually negative. You can then file a BP 9 and BP 10. The entire process can take several months with the extensions always filed by the system, other delays, "lost" paperwork and other excuses. These tactics often are so frustrating that the inmate simply gives up. Rarely is an issue resolved in favor of the inmate.

Rules and Regulations:

You will be given a "handbook" of the rules and regulations as well as the penalties and sanctions for disobeying any of the rules. These fall into the category of 100, 200, 300 and 400 series Codes, the 100 series being the most severe. For example, the 100 code is killing and a 400 Code could be having your shirt untucked from your pants on the way to your job! Each will bring a penalty commensurate with the infraction.

The first will result in new charges, prosecution and a life sentence while the latter will give you extra duty like shoveling snow in the winter or washing windows in the summer.

All rules and regulations will not be covered here but it is important to note the most important affecting your day to day life while confined.

- All inmates must be up, dressed, bunk made area cleaned at 6:00 AM each day.
- Meals are served from one to two hours three times a day.
- All head counts by the C.O.'s (Correctional Officers) are made standing by your bunk. No talking or radios on during the head count. The 4:00 PM head count occurs nationwide every day.
- You must report to your assigned job on time each work day.
- No gambling, tools, knives, pornography, narcotics, tobacco, alcohol, cell phones, computers, pagers, beepers, modification of clothing or tattooing is permitted.
- Clothing not issued or not purchased through the Commissary is not permitted.
- All orders from C.O.'s or staff must be obeyed without argument.
- Inmates are subject to search at any time and your living area can be "tossed" at any time. Any contraband found will result in a write up (shot).
- You are subject to a Urine Analysis (UA) at any time. You have two hours to provide the sample while you are detained by the C.O. taking the UA. After that, if you fail to give a sample you are considered to have "balked" or refused and you will receive a shot. If your UA is "dirty" you will be taken to the SHU (hole) for at least 30 days and may have new charges filed against you.
- All medications must be provided by the medical facility. Pill line is at 6:00 AM and 6:00 PM for those who must have their medications given under supervision, including diabetic shots. It is your responsibility to take these medications as prescribed by the prison Medical Doctor.
- No loaning or borrowing from each other.
- Lights are out at 10:00 PM excepting on weekends.

Of course, this is but a sampling of the very extensive list of rules that each prisoner must abide by.

Prison Hierarchy

The hierarchy generally runs something like this in most facilities: The counselors mentioned earlier are staff. They report to a Unit Manager who reports to an Administrator. All, then , report to the Warden of the facility.

On the Corrections side there are the Correctional Officers who have responsibility for the day to day security of the facility. They are rated much like police rankings. The Lieutenants and Captains are the leaders of the C.O.'s. They are usually union and receive their reviews and disciplinary action from within their own hierarchy unless brought before a prison board. They, then, also report to the facility warden.

Each facility reports to a regional BOP office which then reports to the BOP in Washington D.C..

Security of Facility

All facilities but Camps will have cells, PODS and tiers for housing. There is a lockdown every night. All movements of inmates are controlled. Aside from day rooms, if available, any movement by a prisoner occurs during a ten minute period every hour. The inmate must be at his destination within that ten minutes. His destination might be recreation, medical, a job, the Chapel, crafts, chow hall, visitation, telephone room, the gym or return. Anyone caught in between will be given a shot.

All facilities are surrounded with several layers of chain link fencing, concertina and barbed wire. All have electric fences. A vehicle patrols the perimeter every fifteen minutes or so. The C.O.'s regularly walk the POD, tier and check cells. There are cameras located strategically around the facility.

Cameras are prevalent to watch all activity from a central control, called a "bubble". The "bubble" is an enclosed, secure room with TV monitors, glass all the way around to view the areas and remote actuators for the individual cells to open and close doors.

Each area within the facility has a "bubble" with which to monitor that series of tiers, PODs or wing. C.O.'s rotate duty in the "bubble" If any problem develops in an area an alarm is immediately sent to all on duty C.O.'s and they can be there within minutes to quell whatever disturbance is going on .

If there is rioting or fighting in the yard or recreational area the guards or C.O.'s in the towers can use their firearms to stop the altercation. They are required to use rubber bullets, however, at the orders of a superior, can load and fire live rounds of ammunition at or around the prisoners.

Any infraction by an inmate is investigated by SIS (Special Investigative Supervisor). Rumors of illegal activities, snitches and observations by staff or C.O.'s can result in an SIS investigation. These usually end up with an inmate or two or three or more going to the "hole".

If an inmate is found to be committing violations regularly or if the infraction is severe enough his "points" will increase and he could find himself transferred to a higher security facility. These are more confining with even more strict rules and regulations and tend to be more dangerous for the inmate due to racial tensions and gangs.

All fights and riots result in a facility lockdown where all prisoners are confined to their cells for some period of time, generally one week to several months. All meals are bought to them as well as medical requirements. They will be permitted a ten minute shower once or twice per week. There will be no telephone privilege or Commissary.

There is a no nonsense attitude among the staff and guards. They are not there to be your friend or confidant. Do not think that any bantering about that may go on among themselves or between them and you is a sign of relaxing or friendship on their part. If you take the position that they are always looking for a reason to give you a shot you will do okay in prison.

Meals

The Federal prison system provides meals that meet certain minimum requirements for caloric intake and nourishment.

Breakfast consists of fruit, eggs or pancakes, toast and coffee. Sometimes a pastry is provided. Bacon is rare. Sausage is regular. Cereal is always available along with milk.

Lunch can consist of grilled cheese sandwiches, beans, hot dogs, hamburgers or chicken, a Kool Aid drink, salad bar and dessert.

Dinner can be a stir fry or meat patty, rice, beans, mashed potatoes, gravy and the ever available salad bar and Kool Aid drink.

All eating utensils are made of plastic. All food is served on trays. All drinking "glasses: are plastic.

Inmates working on the serving lines are closely monitored by a C.O. to make certain that all inmates receive a like amount of food, especially the meat and desserts. One serving is all that is permitted on the hot line and, without supervision, a serving inmate will give more to a friend or to curry favor with other inmates. Staples, drinks and salads are readily available on an all-you-want basis.

If in lockdown the meals tend to go from hot to cold because the inmates who normally do the cooking are now confined. The C.O.'s who run the kitchens get lazy and make baloney sandwiches for days at a time.

Major national holidays such as Christmas, Thanksgiving and Independence Day warrant special meals with all the trimmings and ice cream and sodas.

Prisoners requiring special diets due to health or religion are prepared accordingly. It is not unusual for five different food programs to be prepared by the kitchen to accommodate these prisoners. Heart and healthy meals are available at each mealtime.

Work

Idle hands being the workshop of the Devil, inmates in the lower security prisons must work. Prisoners in high security facilities are restricted in movements and work.

Many of the jobs are make work to keep busy but most are repetitive cleaning chores that are done daily or several times a day. With so many men in close quarters cleanliness and sanitation is paramount to good health and well being. Bathrooms are cleaned three times per day. Hallways are mopped and buffed daily. Waxes are stripped, re-applied and buffed monthly. Windows are washed daily in high traffic areas.

Grass, weeds and debris are removed by those assigned to yard work. Snow detail will be awakened at 3:00AM during the winter to remove any new snow from walkways and outdoor rec areas. They will shovel snow throughout the day.

Some prisoners will have visiting room and telephone room cleaning detail. They will clean the offices of staff and their bathrooms under close supervision. They will NOT clean the "bubbles"!

Food service is the most important duty in any prison. The inmates assigned to this duty are responsible for the preparation and serving of meals. They do this under the close supervision of the kitchen C.O.'s.

Food, its preparation, taste and nourishment can cause more trouble in a prison institution than any other issue if not done properly. Consistently bad or ill prepared food will not be tolerated by prisoners. It is in the Wardens best interest to keep the prison population as docile as possible. He does not need the notoriety of riots, subsequent killings and more ACLU lawyers telling the Government how to run their Corrections Facilities and penitentiaries.

Kitchen duty is handled on a three shift basis with the inmates doing the cooking, serving   and cleaning under close scrutiny by the kitchen C.O.'s. Each meal starts from scratch with food cooked or processed in bulk, served, everything cleaned and put away within two hours. The entire process starts again for the next meal within two hours.

Disinfectants are widely used on utensils, all stainless, and floors flooded after each meal. Huge pressure cookers are used for staple cooking (beans, potatoes, soups, pasta, etc.). Large rotating or stationary ovens bake pastry, chicken, meats and other items. Deep fryers cook fish and chicken.

All utensils used in the cooking process are issued to individual inmate kitchen workers as needed and must be cleaned and returned after each meal preparation to the supervising C.O. Any missing utensil results in the prisoner receiving a shot.

If the facility has a UNICOR (Government manufacturing facility to produce furniture, clothing or other items sold within the government system) prisoners with high fines or many years to serve are allowed to do these jobs. For the most part these jobs are coveted more than the others because the rate of pay is usually five to ten times the going rate.

For example, the minimum base rate for menial tasks such as cleaning hallways and bathrooms is $.10 per hour. UNICOR workers can be paid as high as $1.25 per hour. All "money" earned is transferred to the inmates Commissary account once per month which he can use to pay for phone calls and purchase food, stamps, candy, radio, watch, batteries, packaged food products, coffee, tea, soft drinks and many other items. Unfortunately, with minimum pay and no outside support from family or friends an inmate may only receive enough money from his job to buy a jar of coffee each month, maybe.

Recreation

There a various forms of recreation available, again depending on the facility.

The "yard" is an outdoor open area that may or may not have grass. There is usually a track around the perimeter where many of the inmates spend their time walking or running laps. The interior has sufficient room for softball or soccer which are played in leagues during the summer.

Most facilities have outdoor basketball courts.

Many facilities have an indoor gym that has stationary exercise machines as well as basketball and handball courts.

Each wing in a facility has one or more television sets catering to various interests among the inmates. There are many arguments about who watches what and who belongs to what chair or space location.

Crafts are usually permitted such as beading, crochet, leather working, painting, drawing and ceramics. The inmate must purchase his own materials for these crafts through the recreation department and all materials must be stored where used, not in his cell locker.

Board games and cards are standard throughout the entire prison system.

Many facilities have musical instruments such as acoustic and electric guitars, drums, horns and piano. Inmates will form bands or groups and practice for shows that are put on from time to time.

Pool tables and Bocce ball courts are available.

The libraries at the facilities are well stocked with books of all sorts. Legal books occupy a large part of the libraries.

Correspondence courses are encouraged for inmates to further their education. Every inmate without a high school diploma must take GED classes.

Religious services are available for every faith and denomination.

Prison Diseases

All prisons maintain a very high level of cleanliness and sanitation. The isolation of inmates from the outside world is near complete, except for newly transferred inmates into the facility, visitors on visitation day and the staff itself. These are typical ways that disease make its way into a facility.

Newly incarcerated inmates may or may not have been in any jail or prison prior to their arrival. If they have somehow contracted any blood borne disease because of behavior such as homosexuality, using dirty needles when shooting up on drugs or received a tainted blood transfusion they could have hepatitis or herpes. These new inmates use the bathrooms, brush their teeth, shave and eat in the chow hall. Most inmates will not disclose to other inmates the seriousness of any condition that they may have if they are not symptomatic.

If they are in the early stages of a flu or cold when they arrive it is possible for them to bring this into the facility. When that condition is known the prisoner will often be segregated from the general population and placed under observation with the proper medications dispensed to him until the symptoms are passed.

If inmates are housed in facility where contact visitation is allowed the visitors with children are the most likely to bring in colds, flu, and other diseases such as chicken pox etc..

The staff and Correctional Officers come and go each day and they can be a source of spreading any health problems among the   inmates.

Wash your hands frequently and try to use bathrooms and sinks as soon after cleaning as possible. Change sheets and blankets regularly and, if you are have access to a washing machine and dryer, wash your own. Do not use anothers' soap, toothpaste or razor. Avoid inmates and staff who are sick or have a cold.

Medical

The medical department is staffed with a Doctor, nurses and physician assistants. These will administer exams, x-rays, blood pressure, dispense medications and tend to injuries. For issues that go beyond their capabilities or requiring specialized equipment and services not available, the medical staff will transfer the inmate to either a local hospital, clinic or another Federal facility for treatment.

Inmates who require daily medications that must be monitored by the medical staff must go to pill line morning and/or evenings. After dispensing the medication the inmate must open his mouth and manipulate his tongue to the observing medical personnel to assure that the medication was taken and swallowed. As incredible as it may sound many inmates regularly try to hoard medicines that might even remotely result in a "high" or "low" if taken in quantity! Diabetic shots are self administered and witnessed by the a staff member after his readings are taken for dosage.

Other medications required by an inmate made be prescribed and issued for thirty days at a time such as high blood pressure pills, inhalers, ibupropen and others.

Inmates who have a serious onset of a medical problem such as a heart attack, stroke or asthma crisis are treated as an emergency but often the facility is ill equipped to deal with the illness. It has been observed that inmates who suffered a health crisis resulting in death are immediately transported by EMT or ambulance to a local facility where he is pronounced deceased upon arrival (DOA). Even though the inmate expired in the facility his record will show that he died in route so as not to create a paperwork and investigative problem for the prison and staff.

Riots or fights resulting in the killing of an inmate by other inmates or staff are investigated and disciplinary action is taken.

Visitation

Prisoners are allowed visitors on the weekends and holidays. Depending on the facility the visits are contact or no contact behind partitions with telephone communication. There are no conjugal visits in a Federal prison or Camp.

All talking and contact is monitored closely by guards and cameras. Visitors are not permitted to bring in anything of value and no notes or any other exchanges may be made between the visitor and the inmate.

All visitors must be pre-approved by prison officials prior to any visitation. The inmate must submit a phone list and visitor list to his counselor and approval may or may not be granted after verification. No Federal prisoner may have contact with a convicted felon outside, either by telephone or mail.

Visits can last from one hour to as long as six hours if the visitor has traveled a long distance. Again, it depends on the facility and regulations. Children and friends are permitted to visit with the inmate if they have been approved.

A prisoner can lose visitation privileges for months at a time for committing certain infractions of regulations.

Telephone Privileges

Inmates not on restriction have telephone access during certain allocated hours. If an inmate is not able to call collect or lacks sufficient funds in his account to purchase the phone service his counselor will usually permit one short call per month to his family or attorney.

Calls from prison systems pay phones usually cost $.25 per minute but services can be procured by the inmate that reduce that cost to as low as $.05 per minute. These funds come from the inmates Commissary account replenished either from his job or from funds sent by family or friends. Inmates are restricted to fifteen minute calls to allow other inmates to use the phones.

All telephone calls are recorded and reviewed for content. Any threats or suspicion of an enterprise or illegal activity will result in an investigation by SIS and the inmate could be disciplined.

An inmate can lose telephone privileges for up to several months for certain infractions.

Mail, Books and Magazines

All incoming mail and outgoing mail is monitored by the authorities. Photos exceeding 5" X 7" are not permitted and some are not permitted on photo paper, depending on the facility. They must be copied to regular paper by the sender. Photo paper can be saturated with chemicals that might be used as a drug or even an explosive.

Nothing but mail may be received by the inmate. Special medication not available or authorized by the BOP or personal items are prohibited. Reading glasses may be received with an approved frame.

Inmates may receive books and magazines from the outside providing they meet certain criteria. Hardcover books must be sent directly from the publisher to the inmate to assure that no binding contains drugs. Magazines and soft cover books can be received providing the quantity does not exceed a specific number during the week or month.

Stamps are purchased from the Commissary. No stamps are permitted to be mailed to the inmate by friends or family. Stamps are often used for currency between inmates in the prison system. A $.42 purchased stamp has a trade value of $.35 inside. This currency is then used to purchase haircuts, tattoos, payment for gambling, food products smuggled from the chow hall or Commissary products between paydays. This activity is prohibited but is widely done anyway.

Anyone caught with an inordinate number of stamps during a toss or body search will be charged with running an enterprise and will be given a shot and probably sent to the hole.
Mail call or delivery is conducted once per day during the week. Prisoners confined in solitary or segregation in high security facilities do not receive their actual mail. Mail is transmitted electronically from a central location to a TV monitor screen which placed in front of the prisoners cell where he can read his mail from that screen.

Buying and Selling; Lending and Borrowing; Theft

Simple advice, don't do it if at all possible. It is against the regulations and will result in a write up for those caught. It is regularly done by inmates who need something and others who have it to sell or give.

If you must buy something from another inmate you will pay them in whatever the going currency is or some other agreed upon item. If, at the time, you don't have the wherewithal to pay then do not take it on "credit". You do not know what his or your status is going to be when the debt becomes due. If you are not able to pay you could bring trouble on yourself that you don't need. It goes the same way if the debt is owed to you.

There is nothing more despicable to prisoners, aside from child molesters and homosexuals, than a thief or a snitch. Those who are caught stealing are dealt with swiftly and severely. Understand that, once a man has been deprived of his freedom, his possessions, his family and his finances the only thing he has left are the meager items he is able to accumulate in prison and his integrity or word.

Compromising any of these is going to dangerous ground. Taking an inmates belongings, disrespecting him through disparaging remarks or slighting him can result in an altercation.

"Bulldogging" …Rent…Payment from outside…Favors…..etc.

Bulldogging is where inmates, through threat or action, attempt to intimidate another inmate for payment or favor. This can range from demanding monthly "rent" on his cell even though they have no claim to it. In return, the inmate is protected by the parties involved from the parties themselves! While this is more prevalent in detention centers it has been known to occur in the higher secutiry prison facilities.

The bulldogged inmate is expected to pay regularly from his Commissary account. If the inmate is known to have access to substantial financial resources on the outside he may be "encouraged" to supply the Commissary accounts of others with funds.

Sometimes inmates will demand the expertise of a new inmate if he has special knowledge in stocks, bonds or other schemes to make money.

It is important for a new inmate to make alliances with like minded individuals upon arrival. This alliance may be joined along racial lines, ideological line or religious lines. More often than not other inmates will approach the new inmate with the proposition or demand that he ally himself one way or another.

Each prisoner must determine whether or not any of these relationships are beneficial to his safety and well being.

Greetings and Courtesy

Prison culture demands certain protocols and courtesy. Eye contact is selective, usually within the races. All greetings begin with the fist bump often seen among athletes and some entertainers on the outside. Actually, the fist bump is better than a handshake. It is more sanitary as a large number of greetings occur on the way to the chow hall to eat. Refusing the fist bump is considered a slight or "dis".

A "whatsup" or "hey" is a nominal greeting. No one calls each other by name unless they are buddies.

Over time inmates will find their comfort zone within the system. They will gravitate to like minded individuals and nearly always form their relationships along racial lines. They will occasionally mix to participate in sports or games but generally stay among themselves.

Gambling

Gambling, is prohibited but this does not preclude the fact that many inmates do it. Gambling inside comes in the form of poker games, board games and sports betting. Basketball and football pools are rampant during the season.

Payments are made with transfers to Commissary accounts from the outside, stamps and even food products such as packages of mackerel procured through the Commissary. In the course of betting markers are used in place of any form of currency so as not to arouse suspicion among the guards.

All markers and debts must be paid. There is little tolerance for those who welsh on a debt inside. Some leeway will be given on the time to pay off but not for too long.

Penalties are severe for those caught gambling.

Gangs and Races

No writing about a prison would be complete without mentioning the impact of gangs and races in a prison environment. Suffice it to say that everyone has seen movies and television programs which depict these issues up close and personal.

Be advised that it is real, alive and well in any jail or prison. All prisoners are housed pretty much together, regardless of race, creed, color or national origin. They have no way to separate or segregate. Those in maximum security prisons are more restricted in movement and have but little occasion to congregate together. The chow hall and yard are the two most common places where many inmates are able to mix. Those are where most altercations occur.

Because of culture, upbringing and other factors, races are different. Don't let the social engineers and bleeding heart liberals tell you any different. Racial tensions brew constantly in prison. Some of it is because of the type of individual incarcerated. Often sociopaths to begin with they are looking for any excuse to assert themselves and impose their will on others. Any sign of disrespect from another will result in a confrontation and even an assault, without warning.

Prisons are noisy. The most noise emanates from blacks who, for some reason, must be heard above and beyond all others, put together. They slam weights when working out, shout at each other when face to face in a conversation, slam chess pieces and dominos at boards games, slap cards hard on the table at card games and generally disrupt all those around them. This is tolerated for only so long by Mexicans and Whites before an outbreaks of violence occurs.

Mexicans are highly volatile and especially have problems even with each other if involved in different gangs. Norteños, United States citizen Mexicans, are generally identified by themselves
as Chicano. National Mexicans from south of the border, Sudeños, are generally identified by

themselves as Paisans. For the most part they do not like each other, as hard as that may be to believe. They will go off on each other at the slightest provocation.

There are many Mexican gangs. MS 13 originated in El Salvador. Others are from U.S. cities and even communities within that city. Many are nationwide. All are involved in the drug trade or stealing for income.

A short list of Mexican gangs:

MS13 (Mara Salvatrucha)	Surenos
Nuestra Familia	Varrio Hawaiian Gardens Gang
505's	Mexican Mafia (La Eme)
Border Boyz	Los Zetas

A short list of Black gangs

Bloods	Crips
DC Blacks	Acorns
Panthers	18th Street Gang
ii (double "eyes")	BGF (Black Guerilla Family)

A short list of White gangs

Aryan Brotherhood	Skin Heads
Nazi Low Riders	Peckerwoods
Insane Gangsters Disciples 974 PENI	

Alliances are formed between racial lines and often a "gang" within that line. Inter-racial friendships among prisoners beyond simple courtesy and casual encounters is not common practice. Inmates will take meals, work out and participate in sports along racial lines. One of the first things a new inmate learns is where he will sit and with whom in the chow hall.

In the lower security facilities, especially Camps, most inmates are careful to stay out of harms way or be confrontational so as not to lose their good time or even catch new charges for violations. The racial tension exists but actions as a result of it are few and far between. Other issues are more important, especially those related to respect.

Noise

All prisons are noisy. Cells door clanging, shouting, snoring at night, inmates talking in their sleep, C.O.'s radios crackling and cleaning machinery such as floor buffers running.

Radios in prison are not supposed to have built in speakers. Ear buds and head phone phones are sold at the Commissary. Yet, inmates will fashion a speaker from materials available. Round empty oatmeal containers and cardboard toilet paper holders are the most common used to amplify sound from ear buds or headphones.

If there is not a TV room available, all TV sound is off and the inmate can dial   an FM station on his personal radio to listen to the TV through his head phones.

The noise will graduate exponentially as the volume of each radio is increased to drown out one close by. Eventually, other inmates will demand some semblance of quiet and the process starts all over again.

Quite solitude can be found in the corners of the yard during recreation or in the Chapel.

Grievance Procedures

Inmates are able to petition the prison officials if they have a grievance. As noted earlier these are called "kites' (because they go **up** the chain of command of the staff) or "Cop Outs". These are a formal document which the inmate notes the request or grievance and sends to his counselor or staff member. They usually have 30 days to respond. If the response is unfavorable the inmate can file a BP 8 to the next level of authority within the system. If that response is unfavorable he can continue to file up to a BP 11 which is the uppermost authority at regional.

The system typically stonewalls the prisoner on most issues by continually delaying the response. This process can take as long as a year to work through and, even though prisoners have nothing but time on their hands, they will get discouraged by the delaying tactics. Often lawyers are brought into the equation by the prisoner to be their advocate. Sometimes a letter from the lawyer is sufficient to move things along.

For the most part, however, unless the grievance or request is some minor issue such as visitation, or a change of job there will be no resolution by staff. The request will be denied. If enough prisoners petition about the same issue something may be done to prevent any outbreak by the prisoners.
Letters written directly to law makers, judges or the warden are not only discouraged, but against the rules.

Chapel

Religious services or Holy Books cannot be denied to inmates. Even those in the SHU (hole) are permitted to have a Bible, Quran, Book of Morman or....whatever.

The Chapel caters to all denominations and usually has an extensive library of religious books and commentaries. Services are conducted by the Chaplain or an inmate.

Saturday, Sunday and evening services are conducted according to faith and allowed time.

Visiting pastors and Rabbi's occasionally conduct services with permission from prison authorities.

Muslims are allowed to have prayer rugs and to pray throughout the day as required.

Special meals are prepared by the kitchen staff for the various denominational religious holidays.

Native Americans have a space allocated outside for erecting their sweat lodge weekly, wood for fire and rocks to heat. Drums and chanting are part of this ceremony and the sweats last from one to three hours.

Odinists, panthiests and others may practice their faith and rituals as long as no contraband is used in the ceremony.

Homosexuality and other Sexual Activity

With so many men, especially young men, confined in such a small area for such long time the sexual needs and desires of these men are not any different than those on the outside. In the beginning, much like boot camp in the military service, the focus and attention for young men is not on sex but the realization of the discipline, work and hardship. In time, though, their needs are no different than any other man.

Homosexuality exists in any facility. The vast majority of inmates will not have their "masculinity" or machismo challenged or compromised and will resort to violence to any advance by a homosexual. Others will embrace this lifestyle but do so in as much secrecy or discretion as possible. There is little privacy in a prison so rampant homosexual behavior non-existent.

Some justify their behavior to have gratuitous gay sex by being a "catcher" or one who receives the benefit. The homosexual is the "pitcher" who gives the benefit. In the "catchers" minds eye he, himself, is not a homosexual but merely the recipient of a pleasure.

Needless to say, men will masturbate when and where they can, usually quietly in the shower or late at night in their bunk.

Chapter 27

Reducing Your Time

Good Time:

Good time has been covered elsewhere. Good time can only be taken away. Good time is 15% of your sentence given to a convicted felon at the start of his sentence.

DAP:

Some facilities offer a **Drug, Alcohol Program**. Inmates with history of violence or firearms charges are not able to participate in this program.

Eligible inmates will attend regular daily classes related to drug and alcohol issues with the expectation that these addictions can be reduced or eliminated. It's a rehab course designed to make attendees aware of the ramifications of their addictions and how they are susceptible to these addictions.

Many inmates take the course solely to reduce their prison time and have no interest whatsoever in the rehab aspects of the program. The course usually lasts a year with 24 or so attendees per class. After successful completion and passing testing inmates can have as much as a year of their prison term suspended and rolled over into probation on the outside in a half way house.

However, if an inmate participating in a class fails testing or commits infractions of the rules or regulations of the prison, he will be terminated from the class and will not get an early release to probation.

Upon release to probation prisoners participating in the DAP program must continue counseling or AA on the outside for a period of time monitored by their probation officer.

Half Way House:

Half Way houses are established by the Federal Bureau of Prisons to transition convicted felons from a prison environment to a civilian environment. Many convicted felons have served a very long time in prison and require this program to adapt to their new found freedom, obtain a job and start taking financial responsibility.

Convicts are given from a few days to up to a year in a Half Way house located near their homes or where they will do their probation. Half way house time is in lieu of serving in prison. Inmates who have completed Drug, Alcohol programming, been model prisoners and have met other minimum requirements will get Half Way House. Upon transfer to a Half Way House the inmate is now called a "resident".

Most Half Way Houses are set up dormitory style with rules and regulations similar to prisons except for planned and approved movements in society for work, church and home visits. Each person is required to find work and pay 25% of gross earnings to the Half Way House administrators each payday.

All job hunting must be approved days in advance and time outside the facility is closely monitored. Late to or from work will result in disciplinary action. Failure to obey the rules results in disciplinary action. Each resident is required to do some chore within the facility on a daily Basis or will face disciplinary action. Meals are provided but no food is permitted to be brought in by any resident or he will face disciplinary action.

Most of the prohibited items in prison are also prohibited in the half way house. Civilian clothes are worn rather than issued prison issued garb. The inmate/resident must provide his own clothing, toiletries and other personal items.

If a resident commit's a serious enough infraction he will be removed by local law enforcement to a detention center nearby or may even be sent back to prison. All or part of his good time could be taken away and he will serve the rest of his sentence inside.

Visitation is monitored. Residents may, after time and meeting certain minimum requirements of
job and conduct, be able to go home for a few hours up to weekends. Other privileges, such as meals out with the family can be approved after time.

At the conclusion of an inmates good time out date the inmate/resident is released to the control of his probation officer who will then take up the monitoring of the convict during the prescribed time of probation.

Home Confinement

Some residents of Half Way House may qualify for home confinement. This is up to the Bureau of Prisons who still maintain jurisdiction over the felon while in the Half Way House. His Probation Officer must also give approval because he will be monitoring the activities of the inmate at home.

All inmates on home confinement will wear an ankle monitor which he will pay for during the duration of the home confinement. The ankle monitor sends an electronic signal to a transmitter at the home of the felon and should the inmate go beyond the range of the signal (usually 100 feet) an alarm will sound at a central control.

A Probation Officer or law enforcement will respond to the residence and if the felon is gone without authorization he will be arrested and sent to a detention facility to serve out the rest of his sentence. His good time or some portion of it will be taken away.

If you leave a Half Way House or home confinement for any period of time without express written approval from the authorities you will be charged with "escaping". This is akin to escaping from prison as far as authorities are concerned and will bring a five year prison sentence.

The reason you are considered an escapee is because you are still serving your sentence, albeit the good time portion of it while on the outside. United States Marshals will be chartered with securing your apprehension and arrest and you will go back to prison to serve that and any other term that the Court will impose.

Chapter 28

Your Appeal

If someone is convicted, and they feel that the conviction was unfair or unlawful, they can ask a higher court to review the conviction. An appeal can only be based on a legal error. Every convicted felon has the right to Appeal but the Appeal may never be heard or reviewed.

Appeals are filed within 90 days of sentencing unless there are extenuating circumstances such as new evidence becoming available or a new precedent is set by rulings elsewhere that occur long after incarceration. An example of this is the "Crack Law" sentencing guidelines that had been reviewed and modified in 2009 allowing hundreds incarcerated under the old law to be released.

An error of law must have occurred at some point in the process in order for an appeal to be successful. Examples of errors of law include a motion that was improperly granted or denied, evidence that was improperly admitted or excluded, or jury instructions that were improper. In an appeal, the prosecution and defense each file written documents called "briefs", arguing their position.

The briefs are reviewed by the District Court, and in some cases the lawyers for each side must make their argument orally in front of the appellate court judges. The judges then decide whether or not the conviction should be upheld.

Only 3% of all appeals are even heard by the Appellate Courts. Of those, only a handful are remanded back to the original court for review and modification. It is possible for the lower court to impose an even harsher sentence or penalty after review!

Nearly all appeals are denied and/or never reviewed by the Appellate Court.

Remember, all Judges are lawyers and all lawyers are part of the good old boys club. It is rare, indeed, when one lawyer or judge will overrule or overturn the decisions of another. It casts dispersion on the judgment of the judge and no judge wants to have that on his record.

Any appeal rejected or denied by a District Appellate Court may be appealed to the Supreme Court of the United States. The chances of the Supreme Court ruling in your favor are next to nil. The court rules on less than 100 cases per year of the thousand submitted. The Supreme Court's primary mission is to rule on Constitutional issues and those having broad reaching implications.

Chapter 29

You ain't finished yet!
…..or…..
They aren't finished with you!

It is not enough that you "pay your debt to society" by the sentence rendered and time served. You are compelled to generally serve another three years of Probation under jurisdiction of the Court/Judge that sentenced you. While on Probation you will be under the direct supervision of a Federal Probation Officer.

The Probation Officer will require that you see him regularly, require that every aspect of your life is reported to him such as bank accounts, money received and spent, residence and changes of address, programming in one or more counseling or aftercare meetings if required by the Court.

In other words, the entire time you are on Probation you are at risk to be returned to prison for even the most minor infraction. Not reporting a traffic ticket or testing positive for alcohol or drugs can land you back in prison.

While on Probation you must notify every potential employee of your felony status sometime prior to being hired. This notification, more often than not, will result in the employer rejecting you as a potential employee. Finding meaningful employment for a convicted felon is nearly impossible. You will be relegated to the most menial of jobs paying just above stipend wages.

Unless you are applying with someone you know or are looking for a menial job not requiring the handling of cash, entering residences (maintenance work) or handling merchandise you will find it difficult to find meaningful employment.

You will not be able to sell real estate, work in banking or insurance, be a broker in stocks or bonds, work for the Government, Law Enforcement and a whole myriad of other positions.

Depending on the Probation restrictions imposed by the Court at your sentencing you may be required to refrain from the use of any alcohol, may not even go a restaurant where alcohol is the major source of business, frequent any Casino or even go to Las Vegas without prior written approval from Probation.

Continuation of counseling or attending AA meetings may be required for some time.

You will be required to go to a clinic on a regular basis for Drug and alcohol testing through breathalyzer and urine analysis (UA). Failing a UA can result in new charges being filed, revocation of Probation and a start of the entire process once again. Another Probation term will be imposed after serving the sentence on the new charges.

Many released convicts are not subject at all to many of the court imposed sanctions mentioned above. Their probation may consist of reporting once per month to their Probation Officer either in person or by mailing a questionnaire.

You will not be permitted to reside in another jurisdiction without permission from your Probation Officer. You cannot move to another state without permission from your Probation Officer and the approval of a Probation Officer in the other state.

Since 1969 all convicted felons can no longer own a firearm. No pistols, rifles, bullets, gunpowder or any other substance or chemical that can be formulated to make an explosive device. You are not to be able to access any firearm in your residence, vehicle or even ride in a vehicle where there is a firearm belonging to someone else. If caught, you could go back to prison for 20 years!

A WORD OF CAUTION............ *If you are required to have regular urine analysis testing be very careful not to eat anything with the poppy seed as an ingredient. Bread, cake or the seeds themselves should not be eaten during the period while undergoing urine testing. This will stay in yur system for days and you will test positive for heroine. No amount of explaining will deter the authorities from prosecuting you for drug use!*

A released convicted felon is no longer allowed to vote, hold public office or perform jury duty.

Not reporting to your Probation Officer as required or leaving the jurisdiction without permission can result in an absconding charge, less severe than the escape charge while serving in Half Way House or home confinement. Absconding can bring an 18 month sentence by the Court.

\

Chapter 30

No Longer a Citizen

Recidivism

A repeat offence or, for that matter, any offence committed by a released convicted felon falls under the definition of recidivism resulting in a return to jail or prison. The public at large and those In the Criminal Justice System believe and tout that the high rate of returnees to prison is a result of their continued criminal acts. That the criminal is essentially a sociopath who is not capable of leading a crime free life in society. To some extent and with some individuals this is true but not to the extent that the media would have you believe.

The recidivism rate in the United States is 70%! That is to say that 7 out of 10 released felons are found guilty of further criminal activity after their release and are re-sentenced to prison. Because this is true it would seem that the Criminal Justice System and felon himself has failed miserably in rehabilitating himself and has no fear or compunction about returning to incarceration.

Yet the rate belies the fact that a released convict has so many restrictions imposed by the Courts that it is nearly impossible to meet those impositions. John Q. Citizen has no such restrictions to abide by. The convicted felon has a higher standard to live by than any other citizen. He is subject to far more scrutiny than any other citizen.

There are at least 20 million American citizens in the United States prohibited from voting, owning a firearm or any other weapon with which to defend their families or themselves, cannot hold public office and cannot serve on jury duty!

These are released convicted felons from a State or Federal Court jurisdiction and have served at least one year in prison. Many have never committed a violent crime and many more were convicted of victimless crimes, i.e., having a firearm in there vehicle, on their person or not registering a firearm. Others for merely smoking marijuana or using Meth or another drug, or unknowingly passing along a FAX that was sent as part of another conspiracy, and so on!

A man may pursue noble causes his entire life. He may contribute to the greater good in every endeavor. He may be idolized and adored by all who know him. He may provide well for his family and never turn down a friend. He may be a man among men.

Yet, a single lapse, a moment in time, an indiscretion, and act made out of circumstance, a wrong turn or a split second decision will change his life forever. He will be character assassinated, vilified, indicted, arrested and spend a goodly portion of his life in prison, for an act born in the heat of a moment. No one is immune from this possibility. That same man will be always remembered as a ne'er-do-well. All of the good in his life will have been overshadowed by his one act in that moment of time !

In the interests of protecting society and targeting certain individuals or groups Congress has passed laws which ended up becoming "dragnets" for law enforcement and prosecutors to arrest, convict and incarcerate otherwise law abiding citizens. The laws are so broad and often vague that, as you have seen from prior examples, charges can be "stacked" and selectively prosecuted to assure a plea deal or guilty conviction.

People who have harmed no one, where no one has suffered a material loss of any kind as a result

of that persons action, knowingly or unknowingly, have gone to prison for years because of overzealous prosecutors and other prosecutors who have lied, coerced or fabricated evidence or witnesses to assure a conviction. These prosecutors are evil men without conscience or ethics and

have used their convictions to build a career.

As a convicted felon every traffic stop becomes a nightmare. When the traffic officer runs a "Want and Make" through the National Crime and Information Center (NCIC) after they ask for your drivers license and registration they will see that you have a prior felony conviction.

You will then be asked to leave your vehicle, probably be constrained with handcuffs and your vehicle searched. You will be subject to a thorough questioning, What can you do? Absolutely nothing. Your travel will be interrupted for up to several hours while the officer satisfies himself that you pose no threat to society. You will be allowed to proceed without so much as an apology for the inconvenience. That is your lot as a convicted felon.

The authorities are more likely to arrest and prosecute someone with a prior record than anyone who has no prior arrests. Furthermore, any violation of the terms of probation nearly always results in a return to detention or prison where the process through the Criminal Justice System begins anew for the felon.

A "fresh start" is fraught with pitfalls for a felon and he must overcome monumental odds to become a productive citizen after release. Many do resort to criminal activities to derive some sort of meaningful income to live. Remember the drug dealer examples related at the beginning of this publication.

Chapter 31

A Final Word

YOUR BILL OF RIGHTS: Going once, going twice, gone to the New World Order and Global elitists under Jewish Communism!

Amendment I
Congress shall make no law respecting an establishment of religion, or prohibiting the free exercise thereof; or abridging the freedom of speech, or of the press; or the right of the people peaceably to assemble, and to petition the Government for a redress of grievances.

Over time, the most minority of voices in the United States has convinced the ignorant that there is a separation of Church and State clause. As evident, there is no such thing. The Supreme Court has wajjled. on this issue since the 1960 's.

With new hate crime laws being passed freedom of speech is slowly being take away. Political correctness precludes statements, comments or disparaging remarks about people, religion, races and lifestyle without fear of civil suit or even criminal charges.

The right to assemble in public is only granted with permission and/or permits.

There is no longer an address of grievances with any elected official. They are totally unresponsive to their constituency. Congress only does what it takes to get re-elected and expropriate as much money from you to give to others to assure their continued position.

Amendment II
A well regulated Militia, being necessary to the security of a free State, the right of the people to keep and bear Arms, shall not be infringed.

For more than 100 years Congress and the Supreme Court has defined the militia as a Government sanctioned entity such as the National Guard. This was never the intent of the framers and simply subterfuge to impose certain restrictions upon the citizenry of the United States.

The Right to Keep and Bears Arms definition has been so bastardized by the Courts so as to make one believe they are living in the twilight zone! Today, that right has so many restrictions as to be no right at all. The Government can now define what kind of "arm" you can have, how many, where it is allowed to go, who can have it and when. Our right is infringed upon, especially if the Government wants to make an example out of you!

Amendment III
No Soldier shall, in time of peace be quartered in any house, without the consent of the Owner, nor in time of war, but in a manner to be prescribed by law.

So far, the United States Government has not violated this in modern times.

Amendment IV
The right of the people to be secure in their persons, houses, papers, and effects, against unreasonable searches and seizures, shall not be violated, and no Warrants shall issue, but upon probable cause, supported by Oath or affirmation, and particularly describing the place to be

searched, and the persons or things to be seized.

The United States Government, its agents, Prosecutors and local law enforcement violate this each and every day in their pursuit of "Justice". The Patriot Act and Homeland Security preclude these rights under the guise of protecting us against terrorism when they are the real terrorists. Confiscation of private property is rampant in this country by law enforcement and searches are regularly conducted without warrants issued or probable cause.

Amendment V

No person shall be held to answer for a capital, or otherwise infamous crime, unless on a presentment or indictment of a Grand Jury, except in cases arising in the land or naval forces, or in the Militia, when in actual service in time of War or public danger; nor shall any person be subject for the same offence to be twice put in jeopardy of life or limb; nor shall be compelled in any criminal case to be a witness against himself, nor be deprived of life, liberty, or property, without due process of law; nor shall private property be taken for public use, without just compensation.

*Due process mayor not be afforded an accused. The Government can effectively circumvent the double jeopardy clause as noted heretofore in this publication. Any accused not readily cooperative with the Government will receive far more severe penalties than one who is willing to give up his rights to self incrimination. The Government will do **anything** to win a case against an accused.*

Amendment VI

In all criminal prosecutions, the accused shall enjoy the right to a speedy and public trial, by an impartial jury of the State and district wherein the crime shall have been committed, which district shall have been previously ascertained by law, and to be informed of the nature and cause of the accusation; to be confronted with the witnesses against him; to have compulsory process for obtaining witnesses in his favor, and to have the Assistance of Counsel for his defence.

Today, it is common for the Government to detain persons indefinitely without formal charges. Often the detainee does not have access to legal counsel or visitation. The Government can hold individuals while they spend months gathering evidence, intimidating family, friends and witnesses to assure a conviction.

Charges are stacked against an accused with fines and potential sentences so severe that the accused is compelled to take a guilty plea bargain to lesser charges so as not to spend a large part of his remaining life in prison.

Amendment VII

In Suits at common law, where the value in controversy shall exceed twenty dollars, the right of trial by jury shall be preserved, and no fact tried by a jury, shall be otherwise re-examined in any Court of the United States, than according to the rules of the common law.

This is related to civil law. Lawyers derive their income from filing every suit imaginable. The hope and expectation of large settlements for which they receive as much as 50% of any award drives these shylocks with a fervor bordering on insanity.

Amendment VIII

Excessive bail shall not be required, nor excessive fines imposed, nor cruel and unusual punishments inflicted.

Enough cannot be said about the Governments abuse of this. *Bail has been discussed* *previously. Fines are imposed that can never be paid and unusual sentences that never existed 50 years ago are imposed every day by the Courts.*

Amendment IX
The enumeration in the Constitution, of certain rights, shall not be construed to deny or disparage
others retained by the people.

The Government cares not one whit about its citizenry. It will violate the rights of citizens anytime it suits their purpose. Most cannot defend against the vast power and resources of the Government.

Amendment X
The powers not delegated to the United States by the Constitution, nor prohibited by it to the States, are reserved to the States respectively, or to the people.

The Federal Government is encroaching more and more on States rights. If a State resists the Government denies financial aid, imposes certain restrictions and otherwise penalizes the State. Big brother wants everyone from cradle to grave and is moving quickly and forcefully to assure this.

Terrorism

Terrorism is at the forefront of the news. The Government needs Americans to be fearful about something, always! Straw man demons must be created out of whole cloth to focus the attention of the public on everything but the nefarious activities of the Government. Not the least of which are the thieves who have plundered our treasury coffers and our economic future, nearly all Jews and their sycophants. You are suspect if you write, associate with or protest against anything the Government is supporting.

If the authorities search your home and find a fuse for a rocket motor (hobby), chemicals such as acetone, sulfuric acid, hydrogen peroxide, ammonia, gasoline, fertilizer, antifreeze, gunpowder, PVC piping, end caps or anything else the Government has deemed to be materials to create a weapon or explosive (and there are many) you can and will be charged as a terrorist or for having terrorist sympathies and will lose every right as a citizen.

Your charges will result in life in prison and all simply because you marched against abortion, protested the government shenanigans to wherever war it is at the time!

Beware!

Do not associate with radical elements. If you are of the mind to act on your conscience keep it to yourself and do what you are going to do and never, never, never, speak a word about it to anyone. Always act alone, keep nothing in your home or vehicle that can incriminate you.

The FBI will vigorously investigate white collar "criminals" because the Feds are less apt to get their pansy asses shot off. Street gangs, spaced out drug users and drug cartels pose a real threat to well-being of Federal Agents and they rarely go after these groups! If the Government aggressively pursued these gang bangers, major drug dealers and others who pose a real threat to society there wouldn't be so many of them operating freely all over the country!

There a hundreds of thousands of street criminals and gangs committing bodily harm to unsuspecting citizens and the Feds go after accountants, stock brokers, bankers and business leaders.

The Feds are afraid to wage war on the Crips, Bloods and MS13/Mexican Mafia. They would rather sit on their asses and go after those who commit "victimless" crimes such as smoking dope, having a firearm but committing no crime, transacting business over the phone (wire fraud), sending an insurance claim through the mail (mail fraud), and on and on!

Yet they themselves commit TREASON each and every day by refusing to seek out and arrest illegal's from the mid-east, Mexico, El Salvador and every other third world sewer that exists.

They are in collusion with the New World Order Elitists (Yes, Rushbo, THEY really do exist!) and the Anti-Defamation League to remove any potential threat to the agenda of the NWO and that includes you.

Not just the drug users/dealers, murderers, gang bangers and others that threaten the well being of John Q. Public but those who are erudite, intelligent and have a clear understanding of what the rascals in Washington are doing to us each and every day!

The Government does not assent to its own laws or treaties. Countries making treaties or have special relationships with America are on dangerous ground. Our Government will turn on its friends (except Israel) in a New York heartbeat. For those who we place in power in third world countries they are at extreme risk for a short life or plane crash if they stray from policy.

Our treaties with the Native American tribes in the United States are a farce. Not one has ever been honored since they were drafted and signed by the Government. The United States abrogates these treaties which have the full force and authority beyond our own Constitution in the interests of expediency and control. By subjecting Natives on their Reservations to Federal Aid through the Department of Interior and the Natives accepting this Federal aid the Government exercises total power and control over the Native population.

Even though the reservations are SOVEREIGN LANDS to the natives and, by treaty, they are self-governed, the Government regularly sends Federal authorities to demand, make arrests with the FBI, ATF and otherwise impose its will upon the nations. Double jeopardy occurs often as the native nation will arrest and prosecute one of its own and yet the same charges will be bought by the Federal Government and place the Native under Federal Jurisdiction.

Politricks is Machiavellian politics. Machiavelli states that "ruthless cunning is the appropriate conduct for Government!" How very true.

Von Clauswitz states that War is the natural extension of politics. Every President, administration and our unelected   rulers need a good war to feed the military industrial complex and to impose our will throughout the world.

Hypotwits are those who rule over us. We have long forgotten that We, The People are the RULERS, not those who we elect to represent our interests or those that remain year after year behind the scenes actually ruling us. They have infiltrated and hold Government as tyrants pressing against our freedoms day by day. We are frogs in the pot just about finished being cooked!

"Who controls the past controls the future. Who controls the present controls the past!"
George Orwell....Author of 1984 written in 1949!

It is clear to anyone who has lived more than 65 years that America's history has been revised to reflect the goals of the New World Order Elitists. Our national hero's and Founding Fathers have been character assassinated, demeaned, belittled and our holidays turned over to the Black, the Mexican and the Jew.

Our national Christian symbols have been systematically removed from the public consciousness. Prayer is no longer allowed in school and most public forums.

Diversity and Multiculturalism is destroying our morals, our culture and our nation. Hate crime can mean anything the Government wants it to mean but can never be committed against a Caucasian.

Stalin, a great friend of Franklin Roosevelt and murderer of 20 million of his countrymen, knowingly stated that it doesn't matter who votes for who. What matters is who controls the ballot box! How true.

In our last three national elections there has been controversy over the results of the state counts. We all have the image of the man looking near cross-eyed at a torn shard on a recounted ballot in Florida in the 2004 election. It took a Supreme Court decision to declare Bush the winner. Stalinistic Communism is alive and well in AmeriKa.

Some electronic ballot machines were known to have been programmed to direct votes to candidates whether the citizen voted for that person or not. It is common knowledge that illegal aliens regularly vote in our elections. Others seem to be able to vote more than once. With tongue in cheek we say to each other "Vote early and vote often"! This happens more than you might think.

Finally, the President selects unelected "CZAR's" (interesting term) to oversee many of our businesses and Governmental departments. This is cronyism at its finest. None of these Czars are qualified and have no prior experience in these newly created Government jobs.

Each Czar is paid well over $100,000.00 per year and requires staff and offices costing several times that, not including their budgets for travel, entertainment, vehicles and allowances. They are responsible for policy making and even have powers far exceeding any citizen. They operate with impunity and no oversight and report only to the President. Congress has no say in what they can and cannot do, as with most of those who operate behind the scenes in Washington.

For those of you who have read this far it should be apparent that America is doomed as a nation. We have transitioned from a Constitutional Republic to a Democracy (mob rule). It is just a matter of few short years when the economic collapse is complete and new Draconian laws are implemented under the guise of National Security.

May God help you and have mercy on us all! For our disobedience and arrogance he is through with blessing us as a people and as a nation.

Bibliography:

The Constitution of the United States of America
The Bill of Rights
The first Ten Amendments to the Constitution
Title 18 of The United States Criminal Code
Title 26 of the United States Internal Revenue Service Code
Maryland Reporter Citation Series
United States Federal Sentencing Guidelines
Unintended Consequences by John Ross
The Tyranny of Good Intentions *"How prosecutors and law enforcement are trampling the Constitution in the name of justice"* By Paul Craig Roberts and Lawrence Stratton
Other publications credited within the publication.
Legal Match - Provided legal information from the Net
Pittsburgh Post Gazette Investigative Series by Bill Moushey- 1998